Favorite Ways to Garden

FROM GARDEN CLUB MEMBERS

© Favorite Recipes Press MCMLXXIV
P. O. Box 3396, Montgomery, Alabama 36109
Library of Congress Catalog Card Number 74-84082
ISBN 0-87197-068-6

The Montgomery Federation of Garden Clubs

"Hillcrest"   1632 South Court Street   Montgomery, Alabama   36104

Garden Club Members . . .

. . . have always enjoyed sharing their creative and inventive methods of gardening—with neighbors, friends, other Garden Club Members and now with you.

This edition has an invaluable assortment of tried and proven ideas of basic horticultural practices that have worked for these contributing gardeners. This collection will not only be most helpful to beginners planning their first flower bed or landscaping the home property, but it will also be an asset to even the experienced gardener.

From ladies with many, many years of plain dirt gardening come these essential concepts for successful growing of flowers, shrubs, roses and houseplants. Since these hints have come from many different locales, be sure to check your temperature zone before trying any of these projects.

We want to thank each of these helpful gardeners for making *Favorite Ways To Garden* such an informative new gardening book.

Sincerely,

Mrs James Rankin

Mrs. James E. Rankin
Chairman

"HILLCREST"
Home of Montgomery Federation of Garden Clubs
Montgomery, Alabama

Contents

TEMPERATURE ZONE MAP

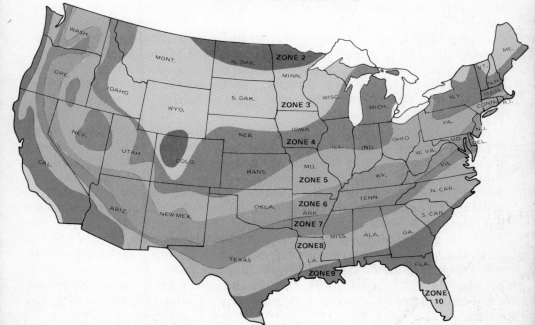

Preparing Flower Beds

Proper preparation of planting areas is an important key to successful flower growing. Plants need optimum space and fertile soil for healthy root growth.

Begin this preparation with an analysis of your soil. This is available through local agricultural experiment stations and county agents. Test findings will indicate the acidity or lack of acidity in your soil and the elements which are needed for plant life.

Plants grow best in loose, porous soil (this is called friable soil). This allows the roots to spread easily but still hold enough moisture to liquify plant nutrients in usable form. Soil which is too sandy will not hold enough moisture whereas clay soils tend to pack too hard for adequate root growth and proper drainage. Since roots also need air as well as moisture, poor soils may be improved with well-mixed additions of compost or humus, peat moss, or a vermiculite-type product or a mixture of any or all of these materials. Adding sand to clay soil makes it more workable.

The best time to prepare your flower beds is during a dry spell at the end of a growing season. Chores needing attention are fewer at this time and the weather often is cooperative and pleasant. Autumn preparation will allow earlier spring planting when danger of frost is past in most areas. Overwintering allows turned under sods to age during wet or freezing weather.

Deep digging of a flower bed is essential for successful gardening. The bed should be dug at least twice the depth of the spade. After the soil has been turned, all the weeds and grass should be removed. Then, turn the bed again. Sand, peat moss and fertilizers can be worked into the soil during this turning. After all the clods have been pulverized, the bed should be raked smooth.

If the bed is known to be infested with nematodes or any other plant destroying insects, it is important to fumigate the flower bed before planting. This can be done by covering the bed with a plastic sheet after distributing a soil fumigant. This gas will kill all weed seeds, soil diseases and insects still living in the soil. These chemicals must be handled with extreme caution and care should be taken to use them *exactly* as directed on package. Please note lapse of time before planting.

Since good drainage is essential to all plants (except bog or pool plants) care should be taken to smooth off, or grade, planting areas so water will not stand in puddles shutting off air to plant roots. These steps in bed preparation will be well worth the time and effort when the gardener sees the beautiful results—gorgeous, healthy flowers producing blooms for the whole world to enjoy.

Fertilizer

Fertilizers are a vital part of successful gardening since most soils do not have nutrients sufficient to produce lush plant growth. It is therefore necessary for the gardener to add these required elements such as nitrogen, phosphorus and potash and trace elements such as calcium, boron and iron.

Of these, three are usually needed in the largest amounts. Nitrogen is necessary for cell growth in stalks and leaves. Phosphorus strengthens the stems and roots, and increases the number of flowers and seeds. Potash (potassium) increases disease resistance, aids in good root growth and promotes better flower color. Complete fertilizers will contain all of these nutrients.

Commercial fertilizers are often referred to as chemical or inorganic fertilizers. This means that they are manufactured from an assortment of ingredients according to a formula with a particular analysis.

Organic fertilizers are produced by bacterial action on organic matter. They include rotted manure, bone meal, cottonseed meal, rotted leaf mold, etc. They condition, as well as fertilize, the soil because of their spongy bulk. Organic fertilizers often cannot supply the strong, quick boost necessary for lush plant growth, but they are excellent for long-range feeding and conditioning of the soil. Fertilizer manufacturers make products labeled for many different kinds of plants—lawn food, rose food, bulb food, azalea food, etc.

Fertilizer is available in dry, granular or liquid form. Some need diluting as per package instructions. Plant foods can only be absorbed in liquid form; dry formulas should be watered in.

There are many types of fertilizers for many uses. One point to be sure to remember—always buy a quality fertilizer from a reputable manufacturer. Follow his instructions and you will have the best results possible.

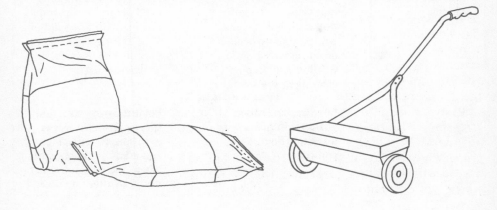

Plant Diseases and Pests

The beauty and health of almost every home garden will at some time be threatened by various destructive pests and/or diseases. The careful gardener can prevent many of these problems by clearing accumulated weeds, (this robs the pests of their breeding places and improves air circulation), and by keeping the plant beds well drained (this will retard moist conditions which can result in fungi).

The following are a few of the fungi and other diseases that can attack the garden.

DISEASE	CHARACTERISTICS	CONTROL
Leaf Spot	dark blotches on leaves caused by bacteria and fungi	Remove old leaves and stems and infected leaves; spray plants at the beginning of the growing season; mulching beds reduces virus-born mud splatters on plants and reduces ground moisture losses.
Botrytis Blight	fungus disease causing discoloration and mold; occurs during humid, sunless weather	Remove and burn diseased portions of plants; keep beds clean; use early spring spray of mild Bordeaux mixture; thin plants for better ventilation; keep foliage dry when watering. Plant resistant varieties.
Powdery Mildew	unsightly fungus that causes leaves of flowers to yellow and wither; usually occurs during cloudy humid weather and on plants growing in the shade	Prone-to-mildew plants need plenty of sun and dusting with fine sulphur. Special fungicidal spray may also be used. Plant resistant varieties.
Rust	fungi causing raised pustules on plant leaves; difficult to control	Plant resistant varieties; spray every two weeks with special fungicides and eradicate host plants where the particular rust needs an alternate host.

DISEASE	CHARACTERISTICS	CONTROL
Wilt	fungus disease fatal to many varieties of flowers and fruits	Plant improved, resistant varieties in soil having been treated with fumigants. Remove and burn infested plants—rotate planting with plants which do not get wilt.
Damping Off	a soil fungi which kills young seedlings by causing stems to rot	Prevention abetted by treating soil before planting or buying treated seeds. Once up, (or just before) spray seedlings or ground with red copper oxide (4 tsp. to 3 gal. water). Control excessive humidity.

PEST	CHARACTERISTICS	CONTROL
Aphids	tiny pear-shaped insects of many colors which suck juices out of new, tip growth, robbing plant of dense healthy foliage necessary for good flowers.	Use of deterrent plants such as marigolds, onions, garlic, chives, etc. Regular forceful water spraying of aphid colonies reduces their numbers as well as the use of nicotine sulphate sprays.
Beetles	a large family of insect pests which destroy the leaves of many plants	Pick insect off plant by hand and destroy. Use deterrent plants such as geraniums and soybeans.
Cutworms	fat, hairless caterpillars of black or brown color which feed on new seedlings	Poison with bait from garden store; protect plants with collars made of cardboard strips.
Iris Borers	moth caterpillars that damage the plant by eating into the stems and roots; can carry disease bacteria	Clear beds of old leaves and stems; spray young plants with insecticide in the early spring.

PEST	CHARACTERISTICS	CONTROL
Leaf Hoppers	wedge-shaped insects of many colors that damage leaves by sucking the sap; may carry virus diseases	Knock insect off plant with stream of water; if problem is severe, spray with insecticide.
Leaf Miners	larvae of certain insects hatched inside the plant leaves which it destroys by eating from the interior	Spray the adult insect with insecticide before they have a chance to lay eggs.
Snails, Slugs & Sowbugs (Polybugs)	members of the Mollusk family, which feed at night on low leaves and young seedlings	Inverted halves of orange, grapefruit or watermelon rinds provide a collection center—lift up and drop into can of water and kerosene. Stale beer in jar covers attracts and kills sowbugs.
Spider Mites or Red Spider	tiny eight-legged Arachnida that build webs on leaves from which they suck the sap and stunt the growth	Knock spiders off plant with a strong jet of water three days in a row to destroy these insects in all stages of their development—Flushing underside of leaves important to reach insects. Spray with insecticide if necessary.
Thrips	tiny winged insects which drink the sap of leaves and buds, causing discoloration and deformities	Easily controlled by spraying with insecticide.
White Flies	tiny white-winged flying insects which suck the sap from plants	Keep plants properly spaced for better ventilation; use insecticide, particularly effective are dormant oil sprays used in spring and fall when temperatures range from 40 to 85 degrees.

Footnote: Deterrent plants are those which insects find unpleasant and should be planted among plants prone to infestation of certain insects.

Tips For Successful Gardening

1. Gardening is a year-round job. Use the "off-season" for studying seed catalogs and gardening literature to aid you in plotting your plans on paper. Thorough cleanup and bed preparation precedes planting.

2. Lay out proposed flower beds, fixed patios, and recreation areas according to your drawings to see if they are in pleasing proportion and scale to their surroundings.

3. Underplanting may be wise on a new property so as to learn how much care is needed to keep your beds growing neatly and productively in a setting which needs weekly mowing, raking and edging. Your lawn, to be effective, must always look well cared for. Placement of slow-growing compact shrubs and hardy perennials are more or less permanent. Their habit of growth should be well known before placement.

4. Calendar your schedule for fertilizing and spraying and stick to it. Apply crabgrass killer, if you have that problem, in the early spring before seeds sprout.

5. Choose sturdy basic tools. Mark them, keep them clean and rust free, and store conveniently.

6. Prepare planting beds carefully and cultivate them deeply. Allow plenty of space around plants to improve air circulation.

7. Plan to spend some time in the garden every day. Do not give weeds, insects or disease a chance to establish a foothold.

8. Get to know other gardeners. Exchange ideas and plants. This will benefit even the most experienced gardener.

9. Keep a calendar record of weather conditions, hours of sunshine, planting and blooming times. This will help in planning future gardens or beds.

10. Keep a garden notebook describing various experiments, layouts of flower beds, and any notes about various plants. Information pertaining to colors, effects of sun, rain or wind and types of soil needed will be valuable in future years.

Tools

The gardener's tool collection may be quite elaborate. But, only a few simple tools are really necessary for most routine gardening jobs. Just remember—it is wiser to buy several of the best available basic tools rather than a large assortment of inexpensive specialty implements.

Garden Flowers

Beautiful and delicate—aromatic and colorful—flowers are the delight of every gardener. Whether this is your first gardening experience or an addition to an already established bed, great masses of blossoms can be yours in only a few short months.

You can choose from a wide selection of annuals (plants which live only one season), perennials (plants which live for many years) and bulbs (plants which store food in their underground portions).

Annuals are easy to grow, inexpensive and they produce a multitude of colorful blooms very quickly. This makes them perfect for the novice gardener. Excellent for filling in bare spots around new homes or new flower beds, annuals also make lovely cut flowers for interior decorating. You can grow annuals from seed or you can purchase small plants from a nursery. Either way, you'll soon have a variety of beautiful flowers in many sizes, shapes and hues.

For permanent garden flowers, you'll want to try beautiful perennials. They continue to flower and multiply year after year with only occasional care from the gardener. These prolific flowering plants come in almost every color imaginable and in sizes ranging from very short (excellent for borders) to very tall (some grow as high as five feet). The perennial is so diverse that your choice is almost unlimited.

Pansy

And, of course, you'll want to experiment with bulbs—those magnificent flowers for all climates, all seasons and all gardens. Bulbs are really excellent for the novice gardener because they can be grown with relative ease and because the beginner can literally plant the bulb and watch it grow. By careful selection, you can have lovely, long-lasting flowers at any time of the year. You'll want to try many different seasonal bulbs—and, you'll really enjoy producing some spectacular bulb blooms indoors during the winter months.

In the following pages, you will find numerous invaluable ideas and hints for making your garden a beautiful success. Read each and every one of these little tips.

Annuals

Red	Godetia Mallow Mignonette Soapwort Love-Lies-Bleeding	Cockscomb Statice Scarlet Salvia Mask Flower Balsam
Blue	Pimpernel Baby Blue Eyes Salvia Horminum Venus's Looking Glass Floss Flower	Love-in-a-Mist Exacum Affine Larkspur Flax Lobelia
White	Godetia Gypsophila Mallow Sweet Allison	Mignonette Everlasting Begonia Flowering Tobacco
Yellow	Prickly Poppies Sunflower Blazing Star Nasturtium	Canary Creeper Evening Primrose Cockscomb Daisy
Assorted	Hollyhock Cornflower Clarkia California Poppy Sweet Pea Toadflax Catchfly French Marigolds Verbena Cosmos Pansy	Candytuft Sweet Scabious Snapdragon China Aster Morning Glory Petunia Annual Phlox Sun Plant Nemesia Zinnia Dahlia

FEEDING ANNUALS

Punch holes in side of 5-gallon can. Mix cow manure with a small amount of soil, then fill can with manure mixture or other fertilizer. Bury can in garden, then plant annuals around can in loose soil. Pour water only in can. Do not water plants on top of the soil. Watering through the can feeds the plants at their roots. Punch holes in only one area of the side of the can to use for watering border plants.

Pat Goodell
Canyon Road Garden Club
Tacoma, Washington

MINI-COMPOSTING

Place a 6-inch layer of soil in plastic pan or bag. Stir in vegetable parings, egg shells, coffee grounds and tea leaves as accumulated. Keep soil moist but not too wet, as too much water causes odor. Do not add meat or grease. Store in securely tied plastic bags for use as needed. May be used in ordinary garden or potting soil.

Mrs. Carroll Leith, Pres.
Yates Garden Club
Alexandria, Virginia

RECOMMENDED METHOD FOR STARTING SEEDS

Start seeds or seedlings in foam drinking cups filled with planting medium, one plant to each cup. Slice off the bottom of cups when plants are big enough to place in the garden. Place each cup in the soil, firm down, then pull up the cup high enough to act as a wind, sun, rabbit or worm guard. Paper may be placed over the tops for frost protection without harming plants. Remove and discard cups when no longer needed, but they are a boon while plantlets are small. The plants look much fresher when started in cups and not disturbed for planting. Wisconsin

has three planting zones. Madison is in zone 4 where the winters can get down to 20 degrees below zero. It is rather unusual to set many plantlets outside until about the third weekend in May.

Mrs. Calmer Browy, Pres.
Wisconsin Garden Club Fed.
Madison, Wisconsin

INSECT AND ANIMAL PREVENTIVE

Use 1 cup unrefined Epson salts to 1 gallon water as a spray on flowers or vegetables. This discourages all insects, rabbits or dogs. The spray washes off easily and vegetables may be eaten fresh or cooked. Treatment must be repeated after each rain.

Mrs. Homer Sharpe, Pres.
Green Thumb Designers
Malvern, Arkansas

DAHLIAS

Specific Variety: *Dwarf dahlias from seed.*
Temperature Zone: *8.*
What To Plant: *Seeds.*
When To Plant: *March and April.*
Type Of Soil: *Any good garden loam.*
How To Plant: *Plant seeds 1 inch deep, 2 feet apart in beds or borders.*
Watering Instructions: *Soak soil once a week when weather is dry.*
Fertilizing Instructions: *Use 1 teaspoonful good all-purpose fertilizer dissolved in bucket of water; water plants every two weeks.*

Other Information: Plants will form bulbs which will bloom for many more years. Cut off tops after frost has killed them. Will bloom all summer.

Mrs W. L. Thomas, Pres.
Althea Garden Club
Lamar, South Carolina

AFRICAN DAISY

Specific Variety: *Annual.*
Temperature Zone: *3.*
What To Plant: *Seeds.*
When To Plant: *After danger of frost.*
Type Of Soil: *Light, dry and not too rich.*
How To Plant: *Plant seeds 1/4 inch deep; thin young plants, setting out 10 inches apart.*
Watering Instructions: *As necessary.*
Fertilizing Instructions: *Very little fertilizer.*
Pruning Instructions: *No pruning.*

Other Information: Makes a nice border; very nice for cut flowers.

Mrs. Don Baldwin
Forget Me Not Garden Club
Johnstown, Colorado

BELLS OF IRELAND

Specific Variety: *Hardy annual.*
Temperature Zone: *7.*
What To Plant: *Seeds.*
When To Plant: *Sow in early spring or late fall. Will reseed itself if some flowers are left to dry on plant.*
Type Of Soil: *Any good well-drained garden soil.*
How To Plant: *Spade and rake soil well. Plant 4 to 6 seeds in shallow holes 6 to 8 inches apart. Cover about 1/4 inch deep, firming soil well.*
Watering Instructions: *Keep soil moist until plants are 2 to 4 inches high. Water during prolonged dry spell if plants look too dry.*
Fertilizing Instructions: *No fertilization needed in good soil.*
Pruning Instructions: *Cutting first stalk of flowers will increase branching.*

Other Information: Likes sunny location on row in vegetable garden. Stems are covered with bell-shaped light green flowers with white centers. Plants do not like transplanting unless ball of earth covering root is moved with it. Can be dried for winter bouquets.

Mrs. Walter Drapala, Pres.
Starkville Town and Country Garden Club
Starkville, Mississippi

CELOSIA (RED FOX)

Temperature Zone: *8.*
What To Plant: *Bedding plants.*
When To Plant: *June until fall.*
Type Of Soil: *Average.*
How To Plant: *In a raised planting bed or in pots that can be moved for transplanting.*
Watering Instructions: *As needed.*
Pruning Instructions: *Not necessary.*

Other Information: Semidwarf in size. May use the plumes fresh as cut flowers or dry the heads for winter arrangements.

Mrs. L. Eduard Breland, Pres.
Arco Garden Club
Laurel, Mississippi

CELOSIA (COCKSCOMB)

Specific Variety: *Tango.*
What To Plant: *Seeds.*

When To Plant: *When weather is warm and settled.*
Type Of Soil: *Sandy loam.*
How To Plant: *Cover seeds 4 times their thickness with soil in a prepared bed.*
Watering Instructions: *Keep moist until well started.*
Fertilizing Instructions: *Fish oil emulsion gives best results.*

Other Information: Keep well cultivated and do not allow to get too dry. Produces beautiful plumes that may be dried for winter arrangements.

Hertha Woodrum
Hartford Garden Club
Hartford, Michigan

GERANIUM PROPAGATION

Make a 5 to 6-inch cutting from new wood that is firm any time before frost. Make a slanting cut below leaf node and remove leaves on the lower part of the stem that will be inserted in rooting medium. Dip stem lip in Rootone. Combine 1 part each garden loam and compost or peat moss. Root geranium slips in the potting soil with a small amount of sharp sand at the base of each cutting to assist in draining. Keep moist. Let stand in a light place where temperature will not drop below 40 degrees. Repot after cuttings root and start to put out new growth.

Mrs. Fred B. Davis, Pres.
Stoneville Garden Club
Stoneville, North Carolina

GERANIUM

Specific Variety: *Martha Washington, regulars, fragrants.*
Temperature Zone: *9.*
What To Plant: *Bedding plants.*
When To Plant: *Early May after frost.*
Type Of Soil: *Rich in humus from compost.*

How To Plant: *In rows or beds with roots below ground level. Make nice borders.*
Watering Instructions: *7 to 10-day intervals in heat. Geraniums do best in rather dry soil.*
Fertilizing Instructions: *Equal parts of bone meal, blood meal and soil.*
Pruning Instructions: *Prune if leggy and plants will send out more branches and flowers.*

Other Information: Plant dwarf or tall marigolds among geraniums and in flower or vegetable gardens to keep insects away. Garlic plants also keep insects from crops.

Agnes Kangas
Dirt Dabbers Garden Club
Shelton, Washington

GERANIUM

Specific Variety: *Maxine Kovaleski.*
Temperature Zone: *6.*
What To Plant: *Seeds, bedding plants or cuttings.*
When To Plant: *Early May.*
Type Of Soil: *Cool, well-drained, moderately rich.*
How To Plant: *Deep enough to accommodate roots.*
Watering Instructions: *Not too much water as geraniums are fairly drought resistant.*
Fertilizing Instructions: *An annual top dressing of decayed manure or rich compost should do.*
Pruning Instructions: *Enough to keep plant of desired size. Cuttings may be rooted.*

Other Information: Can be used for hedges, borders, beds, boxes and indoor potted plants as there are so many varieties of geraniums, offering rich and varied foliage and an abundance of brilliant flowers.

Mrs. Ralph Durham, Treas.
Plain Dirt Gardeners
Newport, Arkansas

GERANIUM

Specific Variety: *Zonal.*
Temperature Zone: *8.*
What To Plant: *Pot plants or rooted cuttings.*
When To Plant: *After May 15.*
Type Of Soil: *Well-drained, light soil.*
How To Plant: *Spade ground to prepare bed, then top-dress with a mixture of compost, sand, 1 cup dolomite lime and bone meal. Place plants in firm soil in shallow hole large enough to hold spreading roots.*
Watering Instructions: *Water thoroughly, then not again until moderately dry.*
Fertilizing Instructions: *Liquid fish fertilizer, as needed.*
Pruning Instructions: *Trim out old leaves and blooms. Pinching off first tips will make plants branch. Cut branch of leggy plant to just above eye and plant will fill out with new growth.*

Other Information: Select 3 to 4-inch top cuttings for rooting. Strip bottom leaves from stem. Mix a solution of half Rootone and half talcum, then dip cut end in solution. Place slips in prepared pots to root. Geraniums grow well from seeds but only 1 good plant may come from dozens of seedlings. However, the process is interesting and well worth trying.

Opal Mickey, State Chm.
Oregon Federation of Garden Clubs
Salem, Oregon

GERANIUM

Temperature Zone: *6.*
What To Plant: *Pot plants.*
When To Plant: *After danger of frost.*
Type Of Soil: *Potting soil.*
How To Plant: *Cover roots with soil. Water, then add more soil around stems.*
Watering Instructions: *Water when needed.*
Fertilizing Instructions: *Mix 1 tablespoon Kenca Sure-Grow to 1 gallon water and saturate soil around plants every month.*

Other Information: To make geraniums bloom, sprinkle 1 tablespoon Epsom salts around plants and water well. Repeat every 3 months.

Mrs. Herman Sanders, Prog. Chm.
Monteagle Garden Club
Monteagle, Tennessee

GERANIUM

Specific Variety: *Galaxy, rosy pink.*
Temperature Zone: *3.*
What To Plant: *Bedding plants.*
When To Plant: *Spring.*
Type Of Soil: *Well-drained garden-type.*
How To Plant: *Spade ground well, then make a hole deep enough for plant roots in ball of soil.*
Watering Instructions: *Water frequently until plants are well started.*
Fertilizing Instructions: *Use special geranium fertilizer.*
Pruning Instructions: *Prune only if plant grows too large to be attractive.*

Other Information: Root slips in the summer to produce more plants for spring. Dig up old plants before frost. Remove all but 4 or 5 stems and cut these stems back at least halfway. Pot each plant in 6-inch pot and place indoors in a sunny window. Plants may or may not bloom but will be ready to set outside in spring.

Mrs. Wilbur Haefner
Klemme Federated Garden Club
Klemme, Iowa

WINTERING GERANIUMS

Temperature Zone: *5.*
When To Plant: *March 15.*
Type Of Soil: *Place a mixture of half sand and half soil in pan. Bake in 250-degree oven for 1 hour and 30 minutes to sterilize potting soil.*
How To Plant: *In a sunny location.*
Pruning Instructions: *Take clippings and start in water.*

Other Information: After first frost, when geraniums have turned brownish, pull plants up by roots. Place each geranium on double spread of newspaper and wrap it up. Place in a cool, damp place until March. After March 15, unwrap geraniums. Cut off 1/3 of the roots and 2/3 of the tops. Repot in clay pots filled with sterilized potting soil.

Margaret Berger, Past Pres.
Sharon Hill Garden Club
Coraopolis, Pennsylvania

GERANIUM
SEED PROPAGATION

Moisten milled sphagnum moss with water, then squeeze as dry as possible. Fill a tuna fish-sized can with moss. Distribute seeds on top of moss and place a piece of glass over top. Plastic may be used, if necessary. Move glass to make a crack at edge of can occasionally, allowing a small amount of air to enter can. Seeds will start to sprout in about a week. Remove seeds, one by one, as they sprout to an individual pot or seed flat of garden soil. The seeds will sprout over a period of about 3 weeks, never all at once. Therefore, do not discard seeds when the first few have sprouted. Remove seeds as soon as a tiny sprout appears so seeds will not get embedded in the moss and be damaged. Seedlings may be planted in the garden after danger of frost is over. Plants should bloom the first summer and may be taken in by slips in the fall before frost. These plants are lots of fun and surprises as you will have geraniums like you have never seen before.

Bertha A. Pike
Garden Club of Garden County
Oshkosh, Wisconsin

GERANIUM

Temperature Zone: *3.*
What To Plant: *Rooted seeds or cuttings.*
When To Plant: *After last frost.*
Type Of Soil: *Average.*
How To Plant: *16 to 24 inches apart in beds or window boxes in full sun.*
Watering Instructions: *Add water as needed. Double floret geraniums stand up better in rain.*

Other Information: Our garden club promotes Twin Brooks as Geranium City and presents a Garden of the Month trophy to encourage planting.

Mrs. Ted Arnold
Milbank Town and Country Garden Club
Twin Brooks, South Dakota

GERANIUM

Specific Variety: *Trailing white, pink and lavender.*
What To Plant: *Seeds or cuttings.*
When To Plant: *Spring.*
Type Of Soil: *Half potting soil and half peat moss.*
How To Plant: *In hanging baskets.*
Watering Instructions: *Keep damp but not soggy.*
Fertilizing Instructions: *Use fish meal until well started, then use 0-10-10 weekly.*
Pruning Instructions: *Pinch off tips to bush out plant.*

Other Information: Hang basket in greenhouse or sunny window before frost. Keep tips pinched for bushy plant.

Mrs. Pat Regan, Pres.
Mountlake Terrace Garden Club
Mountlake Terrace, Washington

JEWELS OF OPAR

Specific Variety: *Talinum Paniculatum.*
Temperature Zone: *5.*
What To Plant: *Seeds.*
When To Plant: *Spring when ground is warm.*
Type of Soil: *Well-drained soil.*
How To Plant: *Sow seeds in small patches in garden; cover with burlap until seeds germinate.*
Watering Instructions: *Keep ground damp until seeds germinate, then water as needed.*
Fertilizing Instructions: *Good garden fertilizer.*

Other Information: The seed pods are as pretty as the flowers. Excellent as a filler in bouquets. Will self-seed in protected areas of the garden.

Nancy W. Kidston
Countryside Garden Club
Vineland, New Jersey

GIANT MARIGOLDS

Specific Variety: *Doubloon.*
Temperature Zone: *8.*
When To Plant: *April.*
Type Of Soil: *Good mellow garden loam.*
How To Plant: *Sow seeds 1/4 inch deep; cover lightly with soil.*
Watering Instructions: *Spray lightly at least once a day.*
Fertilizing Instructions: *Add 8-8-8 into soil before planting. When plants are mature and blooming, work 1 tablespoon of 8-8-8 per plant into the soil.*

Other Information: Thin out to 1 foot apart when plants have formed 2nd set of leaves. Marigolds grow and produce best blooms in full sunshine. Keep old blooms cut off and plants will have blooms all summer.

Mrs. Robert E. Kelly, Bd. of Trustees
Montgomery Federation of Garden Clubs, Inc.
Montgomery, Alabama

MARIGOLDS

Specific Variety: *Yellow or orange blooms.*
Temperature Zone: *4.*
What To Plant: *Seeds.*
When To Plant: *April 25.*
Type Of Soil: *Well-drained medium soil.*
How To Plant: *Prepare seedbed; plant seeds about 1/2 inch deep.*
Watering Instructions: *Water weekly in dry weather.*
Fertilizing Instructions: *5-10-10.*
Pruning Instructions: *Cut the tops out of the plants for bushier plants.*

Other Information: The beautiful yellow and orange flowers make nice arrangements. Plants should be cut at first frost. Reserve seeds for future planting.

Hattie R. Gardner
Plant and Pluck Garden Club
Hillsville, Virginia

DOUBLE AFRICAN MARIGOLDS

Specific Variety: *Double African.*
Temperature Zone: *3.*
What To Plant: *Seeds or plants.*
When To Plant: *Spring, after danger of frost is over.*

Marigold

Type Of Soil: *Sandy well-drained loam.*
How To Plant: *Dig large enough holes so roots are not crowded. Add water, let soak into ground. Press soil around plants firmly. Plants should be placed at least 12 inches apart. Be sure plants are in ground far enough to remain upright.*
Watering Instructions: *Water in hot dry weather.*
Fertilizing Instructions: *Cow or sheep manure.*
Pruning Instructions: *Cut flowers as they fade as this induces more blooms. Save seeds for future planting.*

Other Information: Blossoms may be dried in borax and cornmeal for dried arrangements.

Mrs. Oris Jorgensen
Irene Garden Club
Gayville, South Dakota

MARIGOLDS

Specific Variety: *French marigolds, tagetes, patula.*
Temperature Zone: *4.*
What To Plant: *Seeds, bedding plants.*
When To Plant: *After danger of frost, in sunny areas.*
Type Of Soil: *Sandy, loamy compost.*
How To Plant: *Scatter seeds thinly in well-worked soil; cover lightly.*
Watering Instructions: *Keep plants moist until well established.*
Fertilizing Instructions: *Marigolds bloom best if soil is not too rich.*
Pruning Instructions: *Plants are bushier if earliest buds are pinched off.*

Other Information: French marigolds are 6 to 15 inches in height, good for borders. Taller marigolds are excellent as cut flowers. Marigolds are yellow, orange, brownish-red and warm colors. Compositae marigolds are double flowered and single flowered varieties.

Mrs. K. S. Mahoney, Hospitality Chm.
Rainbow Gardeners
The Dalles, Oregon

MARIGOLDS

Specific Variety: *Drawf, French, triploid hybrids.*
Temperature Zone: *8.*
What To Plant: *Seeds.*
When To Plant: *April.*
Type Of Soil: *Beach sand, seashells built up with compost. Grind horse manure, cow manure, weeds, hay, straw, old pea silage and seaweed. Add broken tree limbs, sawdust and shredded newspaper.*
How To Plant: *Cultivate rows for seeds; place steer manure over seeds. Top with soil and compost. Place newspaper sheets between the rows. Newspaper breaks down into good soil in about a year and retains water.*
Watering Instructions: *Water in dry, hot part of summer.*

Other Information: Plant 100 percent more seeds than necessary. The strong smell of the marigolds keep surface insects away from vegetables. Roots of the marigolds destroy nemetodes.

Pearl M. Anshus, Pres.
Edgewater Garden Club
Bow, Washington

NASTURTIUMS

Specific Variety: *Annuals, gleam hybrids.*
Temperature Zone: *7.*
What To Plant: *Seeds.*
When To Plant: *After mid-March.*
Type Of Soil: *Thin sandy soil.*
How To Plant: *1/2-inch furrow, scatter seeds thinly. Cover to ground level.*
Watering Instructions: *As necessary.*
Fertilizing Instructions: *None. Rich soil makes all foliage, not flowers.*
Pruning Instructions: *Pick blossoms to enjoy as bouquets. Encourages more blooms.*

Other Information: Thin the young plants, planting 8 to 12 inches apart. Plant at least 12 inches from nearest plantings. Ideal for rock gardens or window boxes. Blooming persists until frost. Seeds sprout in 10 to 15 days and blooms 6 to 8 weeks later.

Mrs. Marcus M. Finley, Pres.
Perennial Garden Club, Rose Gardeners
El Dorado, Arkansas

PANSIES

Specific Variety: *Viola tricolor hortensis, Swiss giants.*
Temperature Zone: *3.*
What To Plant: *Seeds.*
When To Plant: *Sow as close to New Year's Day as possible.*
How To Plant: *Plant seeds in Jiffy-7 expandable pots or peat pots filled with Jiffy-mix. Sow 2 seeds to each pot; barely cover with mix. Place in warm dark place.*
Watering Instructions: *Moisten and cover until seedlings appear in about 1 week; water thereafter when dry.*
Fertilizing Instructions: *Fertilize with 5-8-7 type fertilizer solution weekly after 4th week.*
Pruning Instructions: *Pinch out leaves to make bushier plants.*

Other Information: Transfer pansies to cool west window upon germination. Rotate pots 1/4 turn daily. Remove weaker seedlings. Admit fresh air during warmest hours when outdoor temperature approaches 50 degrees. Sink pots in flats of loam and place on protected porch or in a cold frame. Place in garden when frost danger becomes minimal.

Mrs. James L. Pettit, Prog. Chm.
Danforth Garden Club
Villa Interlaken, Brookton, Maine

PANSIES

Temperature Zone: *7.*
What To Plant: *Bedding plants.*
When To Plant: *Fall or winter.*
Type Of Soil: *Well-drained rich loam.*
How To Plant: *Dig holes large enough to spread roots out; press soil down around plants.*
Watering Instructions: *Water when planting and only when dry.*
Fertilizing Instructions: *8-8-8 fertilizer.*
Pruning Instructions: *Pick blossoms for floating in water to produce more blooms.*

Other Information: When plants are no longer attractive, pull up and replace. Pansies are pretty until July when the weather gets hot.

Mrs. Johnnie Allen, Pres.
Caladium Garden Club
Birmingham, Alabama

PANSIES

Specific Variety: *Majestic.*
Temperature Zone: *5.*
What To Plant: *Plants or seeds.*
When To Plant: *Pansies may be planted in early April if night temperature stays above freezing.*
Type Of Soil: *Fairly rich soil.*
How To Plant: *Plant pansies in a bed by themselves. Plant close together in good light, not direct sun.*

Pansy

Watering Instructions: *Water abundantly in dry hot summer weather.*
Fertilizing Instructions: *Fertilize with a balanced fertilizer in May or early June.*
Pruning Instructions: *Remove dead flowers to increase and extend blooming period. Pansies will become leggy about mid-July but if they are pruned to remove long straggly stems they will continue blooming up until early fall.*

Other Information: The vast range of color and showiness in the garden makes pansies a rewarding plant.

Carolyn Rebhur
Cincinnati Hills Garden Club
Cincinnati, Ohio

PANSIES

Specific Variety: *Swiss Giant.*
Temperature Zone: *7.*
What To Plant: *Seeds or bedding plants.*
When To Plant: *Last week of March or first 2 weeks in April.*
Type Of Soil: *Sandy loam enriched with compost or manure in pots. Loosen soil with perlite.*

How To Plant: *Let seedlings gain sufficient size to become hardy before setting out. Plant at same level.*
Watering Instructions: *Never let pansies dry out.*
Fertilizing Instructions: *Feed frequently with mild fish base fertilizer; switch to bloom fertilizer when well established.*
Pruning Instructions: *Pinch all blossoms until plant is well established. Keep flowers picked.*

Other Information: Pansies may be raised in planters to control soil and exposure. Move to a protected eastern exposure as weather warms, keep flowers picked and legginess pinched back for prolonged blooming.

Mrs. Barbara Sampson
Shrinking Violets Garden Club
Kirkland, Washington

LARKSPUR

Temperature Zone: *8.*
What To Plant: *Seeds.*
When To Plant: *Late fall or early spring.*
Type Of Soil: *Garden soil.*
How To Plant: *Seeds may be mixed with sand and sown on top of soil in the same bed with bulbs or other annuals.*
Watering Instructions: *Light watering when the weather is warm until seeds start to germinate.*
Fertilizing Instructions: *Light application of 4-12-12 in early spring. Two weeks later light application of nitrogen.*
Pruning Instructions: *Thin plants to 6 to 8 inches apart.*

Other Information: Plants will produce flowers until hot dry weather. Allow some plants to mature and produce seeds. Let these seeds fall to the ground. Next spring they will germinate.

Mrs. W. Harry Isbell, Chm, Bd of Trustees
Montgomery Federation of Garden Clubs, Inc.
Montgomery, Alabama

California Poppies

CALIFORNIA POPPY

Specific Variety: *Ballerina.*
Temperature Zone: *8.*
What To Plant: *Seeds.*
When To Plant: *Spring or fall.*
Type Of Soil: *Dry, sunny, location.*
How To Plant: *Plant seeds where plants are to grow.*
Fertilizing Instructions: *Fertilize as needed.*

Other Information: The semidouble ruffled flowers differ from the single annual poppy. Plants branch freely and flower with abandon.

Mrs. L. Eduard Breland, Pres.
Arco Garden Club
Laurel, Mississippi

PETUNIAS

Specific Variety: *Comanche.*
Temperature Zone: *7.*
What To Plant: *Plants or seeds.*
When To Plant: *Plant seeds in February or March in hothouse; transplant in March.*

Type Of Soil: *Well-drained sandy soil.*
How To Plant: *Plant in small holes; cover plants deeply. Pinch the tops out of plants to thicken.*
Watering Instructions: *Water when needed.*
Fertilizing Instructions: *Fertilize lightly with 7-6-19.*
Pruning Instructions: *Pinch plants back after they get tall.*

Other Information: Petunias like a sunny location and soil that is not too rich. Plants will yield more blooms if pinched back.

Mrs. Odell Clary, Pres.
Rose Garden Club
Bradley, Arkansas

PETUNIAS

Specific Variety: *White Magic.*
Temperature Zone: *4.*
What To Plant: *Bedding plants.*
When To Plant: *May 25.*
Type Of Soil: *Sandy loam with peat moss.*
How To Plant: *Remove plants from containers in lumps of soil without disturbing roots. Plant in soil in garden; water well.*
Watering Instructions: *Water when soil becomes dry to touch.*
Fertilizing Instructions: *Add nitrogen 3 or 4 times during season.*
Pruning Instructions: *No pruning is necessary.*

Other Information: This variety has produced prize-winning blossoms at county fair several times.

Gayle Bixler
Longs Peak Garden Club
Lafayette, Colorado

PETUNIAS

Specific Variety: *Capri, Crusader.*
Temperature Zone: *3.*
What To Plant: *Bedding plants.*

Petunias

When To Plant: *May 1.*
Type Of Soil: *Acid loam.*
How To Plant: *Deep enough to cover roots well. Plants should stand up firmly.*
Watering Instructions: *Water generously to keep plants growing fast.*
Fertilizing Instructions: *Fish oil for good results.*
Pruning Instructions: *No pruning is needed.*

Other Information: The first blooms appear around June 1st and the growth is luxuriant. The height is 15 inches and stems are sturdy. These are the best petunias for sunny spots.

Mrs. Russell Corn, Civic Chm.
Big Sky Garden Club
Superior, Montana

PETUNIAS

Specific Variety: *Any variety.*
Temperature Zone: *8.*
What To Plant: *Bedding plants.*
When To Plant: *Late October to November.*
Type Of Soil: *Loamy composted soil.*
How To Plant: *Set plants out about 3 feet apart and 5 or 6 inches deep to cover root system.*
Watering Instructions: *Water at trans-planting time; keep bed moist but not too wet.*
Fertilizing Instructions: *Good nitrogen fertilizer with iron is needed about once a month after the plants are established.*
Pruning Instructions: *No pruning is necessary but spent blooms or yellowed sprigs should be removed.*

Other Information: Compost the flower beds well with barnyard manure, sawdust and grass clippings before planting. The root system gets established well during the winter months. There are many blue ribbon blooms from spring into early summer.

Julia S. Hall, Past Pres.
Desert Diggers Garden Club
Chandler, Arizona

PORTULACA

Temperature Zone: *8.*
What To Plant: *Seeds.*
When To Plant: *February or March.*
Type Of Soil: *Loose, friable.*
How To Plant: *Sprinkle seeds on prepared soil. Press firmly with a plank or sprinkle a light amount of soil on top of seeds.*
Watering Instructions: *Sprinkle gently but thoroughly when seeds are sown, then water daily for about 2 weeks. Almost no watering is needed after plants come up.*
Fertilizing Instructions: *Manure or 8-8-8 watered in after plants are 2 to 3 inches high.*

Other Information: Small seed pods form where blooms have matured and dropped off. Pick pods when brown and dry. Crush pods and sift through a close woven strainer. Save seeds for planting next year.

Beth F. Jenkins, Alt. Fed. Dir.
Sasanqua Garden Club
Montgomery, Alabama

MOSS ROSE OR PORTULACA

Temperature Zone: *3.*
What To Plant: *Bedding plants.*
When To Plant: *June.*
Type Of Soil: *Good loam.*
How To Plant: *Press stems firmly into soil.*
Watering Instructions: *Water frequently as these plants are thirsty.*
Fertilizing Instructions: *Use manure as these plants like rich soil.*

Other Information: These flowers give much color to beds near house foundation and are very easy to grow. They reach a height of 6 to 8 inches and are sturdy. Good to use in rock gardens. The plants may seed and come up again.

Mrs. Don Newbrough, Gardener Chm.
Big Sky Garden Club
Superior, Montana

SWEET PEAS

Temperature Zone: *8.*
When To Plant: *November.*
Type Of Soil: *Sandy loam.*
How To Plant: *Dig a 12-inch trench; fill with 8 inches of cow manure and 2 to 3 inches of soil. Plant seeds; cover lightly. As plants emerge, cover lightly with soil. Continue until trench is filled.*
Watering Instructions: *As needed.*
Fertilizing Instructions: *No additional fertilizer needed.*
Pruning Instructions: *Flowers must be kept picked to encourage continuing blooming.*

Other Information: Sweet peas like warm feet and cool heads so they are through when the weather gets too warm. Need plenty of sunshine to bloom well. Must have fence or support of some kind.

Mrs. T. Leslie Samuel, Jr., W and M Chm.
Honeysuckle Garden Club
Montgomery, Alabama

SWEET PEAS

Specific Variety: *Any variety.*
Temperature Zone: *2.*
What To Plant: *Seeds.*
When To Plant: *The middle of April.*
Type Of Soil: *Soil enriched with humus, decayed manure and bone meal. Good drainage is essential.*
How To Plant: *Soak seeds in water overnight. Cultivate soil to a depth of 18 inches. Plant seeds 2 inches deep.*
Watering Instructions: *As necessary.*
Fertilizing Instructions: *Apply general fertilizer when plants are 4 inches tall.*
Pruning Instructions: *Do not prune.*

Other Information: Put supports in bed for tall vines to grow on. Sweet Peas grow wherever adequately cool weather prevails for 2 months after planting.

Mrs. Neil Edstrom
Top O' The World Garden Club
Gunnison, Colorado

SWEET PEAS

Temperature Zone: *9.*
What To Plant: *Seeds.*
When To Plant: *January.*
Type Of Soil: *Friable.*
How To Plant: *Dig trench 10 inches deep,*

then add 2 inches good garden soil mixed with steam-dried manure.

Watering Instructions: *As needed.*

Fertilizing Instructions: *Once a week with blood meal, then water often after vines begin to run well.*

Pruning Instructions: *Cut flowers every day to keep vines blooming.*

Other Information: Seed should be placed in trench about 1 inch apart and covered lightly with good garden soil. As plants emerge cover lightly with soil. Continue until trench is filled, then allow seedlings to grow up and begin to climb on chicken wire support.

Mrs. W. C. Goode
Sea Pines Garden Club
Hilton Head Island, South Carolina

SWEET PEAS

Temperature Zone: *8.*
What To Plant: *Seeds.*
When To Plant: *Late fall.*
Type Of Soil: *Well-drained good garden soil.*
How To Plant: *Plant seeds in a trench and carefully spread soil over the seedlings as they grow until the trench is filled. Mulch with straw during the winter months.*
Watering Instructions: *Require frequent watering. Plants thrive in a cool moist climate.*
Fertilizing Instructions: *Light application of general garden fertilizer every 3 weeks.*

Other Information: Vines need to be grown on a fence or stakes with strings attached. Will grow 6 to 8 feet tall. Pick blooms as soon as mature so that seeds will not be produced instead of blooms.

Mrs. W. Harry Isbell, Bd. of Trustees Chm.
Montgomery Fed. of Garden Clubs, Inc.
Montgomery, Alabama

SWEET PEAS

Specific Variety: *Regular large sweet peas.*

Temperature Zone: *3.*
What To Plant: *Seeds.*
When To Plant: *Best planted in fall or as early in spring as possible.*
Type Of Soil: *Any type.*
How To Plant: *Prepare soil by digging a trench 1 1/2 to 2 feet deep. Fill 1 foot of trench with well-rotted manure or compost. Completely fill trench with mixture of fertile top soil and bone meal. Sow seeds 1 to 2 inches apart. Cover with about 3 inches of hay or straw as soon as the ground freezes. Remove hay in spring. Put supports in place when plants are several inches high.*
Watering Instructions: *Water frequently. Watering trenches may be dug on each side of seed trench. Mulch also helps retain moisture.*
Pruning Instructions: *Keep blossoms picked to keep vines from forming seed pods. The more sweet peas picked the more blossoms form.*

M. Fehrenbach
Bretton Woods Garden Club
Lansing, Michigan

MOONFLOWER OR IPOMOEA

Temperature Zone: *8.*
When To Plant: *Plant seeds in pots early; transplant outside when frost is over.*
Type Of Soil: *Rich moist soil.*
How To Plant: *Full sun is preferable but at least half a day is essential.*
Watering Instructions: *Plenty of water.*
Fertilizing Instructions: *Liquid fertilizer about once a month.*

Other Information: The night-blooming morning glory is grown as a perennial in the south and as an annual in the north. Vines grow fast. The white blooms open quite suddenly in the evening and have a heavenly fragrance. Growth to 10 feet.

Mrs. Herman McDuffie, Fed. Dir.
Canterbury Bells
Montgomery, Alabama

Garden of Annuals and Perennials

ZINNIAS

Specific Variety: *Hardy annual.*
Temperature Zone: *3.*
What To Plant: *Seeds.*
When To Plant: *After danger of frost.*
How To Plant: *Plant 1/4 inch deep; thin young plants to 1 foot apart.*
Watering Instructions: *Plenty of water.*
Fertilizing Instructions: *Manure as needed.*

Other Information: Zinnias make very nice cut flowers or background flowers.

Mrs. Pete Grott
Forget-Me-Not Garden Club
Johnstown, Colorado

ZINNIAS

Temperature Zone: *7.*
What To Plant: *Seeds.*
When To Plant: *About April 15.*
Type Of Soil: *Adobe clay.*
How To Plant: *Plant zinnia seeds in rows; cover with 1/4 inch finely powdered soil.*
Watering Instructions: *Water every 2 weeks when first planted.*
Fertilizing Instructions: *Fertilize once or twice with 16-20-0 before watering.*

Mrs. Cecil Ginanni
Garden Dept of Carlsbad Woman's Club
Carlsbad, New Mexico

Perennials

TALL (3 Feet and Taller)		
Columbine Hybrids **	Hollyhock	Babies' Breath
Oriental Poppy	Bellflower	Summer Phlox
Delphinium	Bee Balm **	Blue Sage
Lupine	Heliopsis	Japanese Anemone **
Salvia Haematodes	Lythrum **	Autumn Monkshood
MEDIUM (2 to 3 Feet)		
Aster	Honesty	Daisy
Sweet William	Coreopsis	Maltese Cross **
Jacob's Ladder **	Marguerite	Goldflower
Day Lily	Canterbury Bell	Chrysanthemum
Bleeding Heart **	Astilbe **	Carnation
Coneflower	Foxglove	Plantain Lily **
SHORT (Under 2 Feet)		
Border Pink	Sea Pink	Lavender
Forget-me-not	Wallflower	Goldenrod
Iceland Poppy	Blue Flax	Dwarf Aster
Coral Bells **	Lilac	Balloon Flower
**** Shade Tolerant Perennials**		

HARDY PHLOX

Specific Variety: *Any variety.*
What To Plant: *By division.*
When To Plant: *Fall or spring.*
Type Of Soil: *Well-drained, deeply spaded, enriched with organic fertilizer.*
How To Plant: *Set plants 10 inches apart in sunny location.*
Watering Instructions: *Let hose run slowly on ground; never wet foliage or flowers to prevent mildew.*
Fertilizing Instructions: *Organic plant food.*

Pruning Instructions: *Break heads off as they go to seed to encourage new flower heads.*

Other Information: Phlox is one of the best plants in a perennial border. Blooms all summer and into fall. Has a large range of color. Lift and divide every 3 years to produce large flower heads. Sprinkle sulphur around base of plants in early spring to prevent mildew.

Mrs. J. E. Bowman, Sr., Pres.
Forest Heights Garden Club
Little Rock, Arkansas

ASTILBE

Specific Variety: *Pink, wine-red or white feathery flower.*
Temperature Zone: *8.*
What To Plant: *Divided bedding plant clumps.*
When To Plant: *Spring.*
Type Of Soil: *Well-drained soil.*
How To Plant: *Dig holes a little larger than clumps; loosen soil on clumps and plant.*
Watering Instructions: *Water well when first divided, then regularly.*
Fertilizing Instructions: *Any garden type plant food.*
Pruning Instructions: *Cut back spent flowers to keep fern-like foliage neat.*

Other Information: A sharp knife is needed to cut clumps apart. Fern-like foliage is useful in arrangements after flowers have bloomed.

Mrs. Phyllis Chase, Pres.
Valleyvue Garden Club
Bellevue, Washington

BUTTERFLY WEED (ASCLEPIAS TUBEROSA)

Specific Variety: *Asclepiadaceae, orange to red.*
Temperature Zone: *4.*
What To Plant: *Plants from nursery or seeds.*
When To Plant: *Spring.*
Type Of Soil: *Sandy well-drained soil.*
How To Plant: *Be careful not to break the long taproots of the young plant. Set out in deep holes.*
Watering Instructions: *Water as needed.*
Fertilizing Instructions: *Well-rotted compost.*

Other Information: May be used as a nice specimen plant. Cut freely for arrangements. Cut to ground after first frost. Only true orange perennial wild flower resembling milkweed. Leaves grow alternately on the stem instead of opposite.

Blooms from June to September on new growth each year. Sensitive to herbicides.

Mrs. Florence M. Deason, Past Pres.
Lilies of the Valley Garden Club
Sutherland, Nebraska

STACHYS BETONICA

Specific Variety: *Grandiflora.*
What To Plant: *Bedding plants.*
When To Plant: *Spring or autumn.*
Type Of Soil: *Good ordinary soil. Preferably sunny location but will tolerate partial shade.*
How To Plant: *Best grown in groups of 3 or more. Plant 4 to 6 inches apart.*
Watering Instructions: *Minimum of water.*
Fertilizing Instructions: *Minimum of fertilizer.*

Other Information: Bright purple flowers on 2 to 3 foot stems. Rich attractive foliage.

Mrs. Mildred H. Frerichs
Paintbrush Garden Club
Casper, Wyoming

BEE-BALM (MONARDA)

Temperature Zone: *9.*
What To Plant: *Seeds.*
When To Plant: *Spring.*
Type Of Soil: *Well-drained sandy soil.*
How To Plant: *Cover seeds lightly with soil in bed.*
Watering Instructions: *Water regularly.*
Fertilizing Instructions: *Very little.*

Other Information: The leaves have a minty fragrance. Blossoms attract hummingbirds and bees. Blooms from spring until fall and will grow in shade as well as sun.

Mrs. M. H. Morris, Pres.
Leaburg Garden Club
Leaburg, Oregon

BUGLEWEED (AJUGA)

Temperature Zone: *8.*
What To Plant: *Young plants.*
When To Plant: *Propagate in fall or spring.*
Type Of Soil: *Garden soil or rock garden.*
How To Plant: *Divide old plants. Set new shoots in shallow ground.*
Watering Instructions: *Water often as plants like moist soil.*
Pruning Instructions: *May need thinning in spring.*

Other Information: These plants have dark bronze to purple foliage and blue flowers. They flourish in almost any situation and are easy to cultivate.

Mrs. Stan Baxter, Fin. Dir.
Dixie Diggers
Montgomery, Alabama

CHRISTMAS OR LENTEN ROSE (HELLEBORUS)

Specific Variety: *Helleborus Foetidus, Niger, Orientalis.*
Temperature Zone: *6.*
What To Plant: *2nd or 3rd year plants.*
When To Plant: *Spring or early fall.*
Type Of Soil: *Retentive loam, freely mixed with leaf mold and rotted manure.*
How To Plant: *Plants will have an earth ball and should be replaced at the former growing level.*
Watering Instructions: *Water when planted to settle the soil and during the summer if very dry.*
Fertilizing Instructions: *Top dress with rotted manure and humus each autumn.*

Other Information: Select a shady moist location protected from the winter wind. Set plants out where they will not be disturbed. Plants have been known to prosper in the same place for 100 years. Niger is the Christmas Rose, Orientalis is the rosy-colored Lenten Rose. Foetidus is different from the other two in that there are no basal leaves. Foetidus throws a stalk in late spring that will develop into a 50-bloom head of green flowers the following winter.

Mrs. Chester H. Cain
Cincinnati Hills Garden Club
Cincinnati, Ohio

CANTERBURY BELLS

Specific Variety: *Singles and doubles.*
Temperature Zone: *6.*
What To Plant: *Seeds or bedding plants.*
When To Plant: *Sow seeds in June.*
Type Of Soil: *Any well-drained soil.*
How To Plant: *Transplant young plants in partial shade. Sprinkle with Hyponex or Miracle-Gro mixed in water.*
Watering Instructions: *Water moderately.*
Fertilizing Instructions: *Feed with water soluble plant food.*

Other Information: Pinch fading blooms off at the base so small auxiliary flower buds will develop. Flowering period may be considerably prolonged.

Mrs. Rex Rainbolt, VP
Terrace Tillers Garden Club
Spokane, Washington

CHRYSANTHEMUM

Specific Variety: *Shasta daisy.*
Temperature Zone: *5.*
What To Plant: *Cuttings.*
When To Plant: *May.*
Type Of Soil: *Ordinary well-cultured garden soil.*
Watering Instructions: *Often.*
Fertilizing Instructions: *Decayed manure.*

Other Information: In July when plant is about 8-inches high pinch halfway back. Lift clumps from garden in early fall. Separate and reroot for next planting.

Mrs. Forrest Dillar, Pres.
Guyan Garden Club
Kitts Hill, Ohio

CHRYSANTHEMUMS

Specific Variety: *Japanese, large exhibition.*
Temperature Zone: 7.
What To Plant: *Cuttings taken from root stock, rooted in flats and transplanted to outdoor beds.*
When To Plant: *May.*
Type Of Soil: *Garden loam enriched with peat moss and trace minerals.*
How To Plant: *24 to 29 inches apart, staked for support as they grow. Pinch out growing tips twice.*
Watering Instructions: *Overhead sprinkling until buds get heavy, then at ground level only to avoid mildew.*
Fertilizing Instructions: *Feed often with bone meal, blood meal, seaweed, fish concentrate.*
Pruning Instructions: *Early removal of laterals and excess new starts in weekly work sessions.*

Other Information: Only 4 to 6 branches should be left on the 12 to 15-inch plant. These will yield good quality large blossoms as the plant grows to 3 or 4 feet. Keep the new starts removed. It is important to try for only one blossom per lateral. The plant will keep trying to develop more.

Mrs. Orlan Ice
Ramblin Rows Garden Club
Portland, Oregon

CHRYSANTHEMUMS

Specific Variety: *Perennial disbuds.*
Temperature Zone: *8.*
What To Plant: *Half mature rooted side shoots of a clump or 2 to 6-inch rooted cuttings.*
When To Plant: *Middle of May.*
Type Of Soil: *Well-drained good garden soil with peat moss spaded into the bed and a top dressing of well-rotted manure.*
How To Plant: *Plant in area that receives sunshine at least 2/3 of the day, but with some shade during the heat of the day. Dig hole large enough for each plant root, then place a small handfull of bone meal in hole. Cover with thin layer of soil. Place plant in hole and firm soil about roots.*
Watering Instructions: *Deep watering only when needed. Do not keep soil soggy. Never let plants go into night with wet foliage.*
Fertilizing Instructions: *Fertilizers low in nitrogen are best.*
Pruning Instructions: *After cuttings produce 6 or 8 new sturdy leaves, pinch out tip. Repeat with each new shoot until the last of June for strong bushy plants.*

Other Information: When taking cuttings from clumps, cut stems using a sharp knife. Dip cut ends in Rootone and plant in a mixture of sharp sand and peat moss. For large flowers pinch out tip to make plant branch, then leave only 1 to 4 lateral shoots growing to produce flowers. A cluster of buds will appear. Pinch out all but 2 buds. One week to 10 days later select the strongest bud and pinch out the weaker one. Hope that nothing happens to the remaining bud for this beauty is the price of all the work.

Mrs. Lyle Bayne, State Chm., State Fair
Oregon Federation of Garden Clubs
Salem, Oregon

CHRYSANTHEMUMS

Temperature Zone: *6.*
What To Plant: *Separated old plants or cuttings.*
When To Plant: *Latter part of May.*
Type Of Soil: *Good garden soil or sandy loam.*
How To Plant: *Pinch top of plants back to about 8 inches and plant about 4 inches deep.*
Watering Instructions: *Water well when fairly dry.*
Fertilizing Instructions: *Use nitrogen fertilizer at planting. Use a balanced fertilizer in about 6 weeks. Add some phosphate and potash when buds begin to form to help blooms and bring out color.*
Pruning Instructions: *Tips must be pinched when planted to make plants branch.*

Other Information: If the mums are large like Harvest mums, save the largest bud and remove the small ones on the side of the stem, making 1 lovely blossom. The pompon type does not need as much pinching as the flowers are naturally smaller. Some pinching is beneficial for all varieties.

F. Davis, Sec.
Growing Pains Garden Club
Spokane, Washington

CHRYSANTHEMUMS

Specific Variety: *Early flowering and medium fall mums, all colors.*
Temperature Zone: *4.*
What To Plant: *Divide all old plants and discard woody parts. Keep only best green shoots for planting.*
When To Plant: *As soon as shoots are 2 to 3 inches high.*
Type Of Soil: *Good loamy soil.*
How To Plant: *Set young plants 1 inch deeper than they formerly grew. Slips without roots can be started under glass jars.*
Watering Instructions: *Water well when planted, then water as needed.*
Fertilizing Instructions: *A good application of manure worked around plants. A good soluble fertilizer may be used.*
Pruning Instructions: *Cut plants back after stems are frozen.*

Other Information: When plants are 5 inches high cut or snip off the tops. After plant has grown 2 more inches snip ends again to make plants thick and bushy. Plants can be potted to take into the house where they will bloom beautifully. Spray with a good rose spray to keep mildew and pests off.

Mrs. Clarence Ries, VP
Newaygo Garden Club
Newaygo, Michigan

CHRYSANTHEMUMS

Specific Variety: *Garden, Cushion.*
Temperature Zone: *5.*
What To Plant: *Divided old plants and rooted cuttings.*
When To Plant: *May, June, 1st part of July.*
Type Of Soil: *Good garden soil with good drainage.*
How To Plant: *12 to 18 inches apart or closer if variety is to be disbudded.*
Watering Instructions: *Never allow to dry out.*
Fertilizing Instructions: *Enrich soil with compost, old manure and superphosphate plus 6-10-4 before planting.*
Pruning Instructions: *When plants are about 8 inches tall, cut out top 1 inch to allow plant to branch.*

Other Information: Garden varieties are best divided every year using the more tender outer edges, discarding the older parts. Cushion may be divided every 2nd or 3rd year. Place divided plants in prepared hole and sprinkle roots with a small amount of sharp sand. Water with liquid root starter.

Mrs. H. Hausknecht
Flora Culture Garden Club
Midvale, Utah

CHRYSANTHEMUMS

Specific Variety: *Giant English.*
What To Plant: *Bedding plants.*
When To Plant: *July.*
Type Of Soil: *Fairly heavy soil.*
How To Plant: *Place 4 inches of barnyard manure in flower bed; cover with 2 inches of heavy soil. Set plants out 3 inches deep and 12 inches apart.*
Watering Instructions: *Water when planted and when blooming.*
Fertilizing Instructions: *Barnyard manure, 5-10-5.*
Pruning Instructions: *Pinch 1 inch of the top out when the plants are 10 inches tall.*

Other Information: Flowers will bloom until frost. Remove buds, leaving one bud to each stem.

Mrs. Harry S. Wheeler, Memshp.
Hernando Civic Garden Club
Hernando, Mississippi

CHRYSANTHEMUMS

Specific Variety: *All varieties.*
Temperature Zone: *8.*

What To Plant: *Bedding plants.*
When To Plant: *1st of June, July or August.*
Type Of Soil: *Well-drained, loose soil.*
How To Plant: *3 to 4 inches deep.*
Watering Instructions: *Immediately after planting and every 3rd day.*
Fertilizing Instructions: *Fertilize according to soil needs in spring and late fall.*

Other Information: To transplant, pinch stem to within 6 inches of soil level on the 1st day of June, July or August. Dip cut ends into Rootone. Place 3 cuttings into newly dug holes, then cover with dirt and pack to keep stems sturdy. Water well. All varieties attempted have re-rooted well.

Mrs. Glenn Watts
Cherokee Garden Club
Knoxville, Tennessee

CHRYSANTHEMUMS

Specific Variety: *Football mums.*
Temperature Zone: *4.*
What To Plant: *Perennial bedding plants.*
When To Plant: *Spring.*
Type Of Soil: *Black loam.*

How To Plant: *Small plants 10 to 12 inches apart.*
Watering Instructions: *Water frequently until plants are established, then water at least once a week or when dry.*
Fertilizing Instructions: *As needed.*
Pruning Instructions: *Pinch off buds as they appear until about middle of June. This makes plants become bushy and strong.*

Other Information: Chrysanthemums are fall flowers and bloom until hard frost. Thin out in spring and replant in other areas, if desired, but always pinch off buds.

Mrs. Otto Hamann, VP
Leigh Garden Club
Leigh, Nebraska

CHRYSANTHEMUMS

Specific Variety: *Garden and show.*
Temperature Zone: *4.*
What To Plant: *Cuttings or specimens rooted from edges of old plants.*
When To Plant: *Late April or May.*
Type Of Soil: *Mixture of good garden soil and peat moss.*
How To Plant: *Root cuttings in clean sand. Set rooted plants in garden. Cut bottoms from plastic jugs and place 1 jug over each plant. Remove lids and let jugs remain over plants for 1 to 2 weeks or until well established. These jugs may be kept over fragile plants during winter.*
Watering Instructions: *Keep moist for several days then water weekly.*
Fertilizing Instructions: *Bone meal when planting, then apply Ortho-Gro every 2 weeks starting in middle of June.*
Pruning Instructions: *Pinch off growing tips when plants are 4 to 6 inches high, then pinch off again on 1st to 10th of June, June 20th and July 5th or until buds form.*

Mrs. Kenneth W. Sadler
Dist., State Conservation Chm.
Early Morning Gardeners Club
Nampa, Idaho

CHRYSANTHEMUMS

Specific Variety: *All kinds.*
Temperature Zone: *4.*
What To Plant: *Separated old plants.*
When To Plant: *Either spring or fall.*
Type Of Soil: *Good garden soil with good drainage.*
How To Plant: *Press soil firmly around plants. A small amount of 5-20-20 may be mixed in soil, if desired.*
Water Instructions: *After planting and as needed.*
Fertilizing Instructions: *At planting. Bone meal may be worked into soil around plant, if desired.*
Pruning Instructions: *Pinch out tops to make plants branch into better shape, only up to July 1st.*

Other Information: Water plants in the morning so the leaves dry off and will not mildew as often happens when watered at night. Treat frequently with chrysanthemum dust. In fall, cut stems off 3 or 4 inches above ground and place branches over tops of plants. This prevents ice freezing solid and smothering out plants.

Mrs. A. D. Kellogg
Homer Garden Club
Homer, Michigan

Potted Chrysanthemums

CHRYSANTHEMUMS

Specific Variety: *Assorted.*
What To Plant: *4 to 6-inch cuttings.*
When To Plant: *Late spring.*
Type Of Soil: *Coarse sand, compost, garden soil.*
How To Plant: *Loosen soil to a depth of 6 inches. Add organic material annually, 1 to 2 pounds of 8-8-8 per 100 square feet, working into soil. Set out plants 3 to 4 inches deep in warm moist location.*
Watering Instructions: *Water thoroughly when needed.*
Fertilizing Instructions: *Apply 1 to 1 1/2 pounds of 8-8-8 or 10-6-4 after plants start to grow. Repeat monthly.*
Pruning Instructions: *Pinch the plants back when new growth reaches 3 or 4 inches. Continue pinching back until the 1st week in July.*

Other Information: Remove all except 2 or 3 buds around the center or crown bud if larger blossoms are desired. Tall or weak plants should be staked and protected from winds and heavy rains. Brown spots on leaves may be controlled by spraying Captan at 7 to 10-day intervals.

Mrs. Lillie R. Morgan, VP
Montpelier-Pine Garden Club
Amite, Louisiana

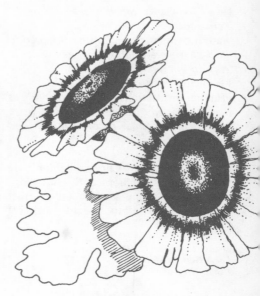

Chrysanthemums

COLUMBINES

Specific Variety: *McKana.*
What To Plant: *Seeds.*
When To Plant: *After the ground is warm.*
Type Of Soil: *Black rich woods dirt.*
How To Plant: *Sow the seeds in a prepared bed in the shade. Cover with mesh or thinly-woven cloth to keep seeds from washing. Keep wet with a fine mist until the seeds sprout.*
Watering Instructions: *As needed.*
Fertilizing Instructions: *Feed with commercial fertilizer until plants are large enough to transplant.*

Other Information: Plants will reseed and come up in unexpected places.

Mrs. J. C. Edwards
Clarksville Garden Club
Clarksville, Tennessee

CORAL BELLS

Temperature Zone: *7.*
What To Plant: *Bedding plants.*
When To Plant: *Early spring or fall.*
Type Of Soil: *Rich soil.*
How To Plant: *Plant in shallow holes, roots divided in clumps.*
Watering Instructions: *Frequent watering at planting time.*
Fertilizing Instructions: *Any light fertilizer, a little cottonseed meal in the fall.*
Pruning Instructions: *When plants get too large, divide by pulling apart and separating.*

Other Information: A border of coral bells is attractive around roses.

Mrs. Mackenson Ellis
Mt View Garden Club
Jonesboro, Tennessee

CORAL BELLS (HEUCHERA)

Temperature Zone: *6.*
What To Plant: *Plants.*
When To Plant: *Spring.*
Type Of Soil: *Rich well-drained sand or loam.*
How To Plant: *Plant in border 6 to 8 inches apart. Place stems in ground to the first leaf.*
Watering Instructions: *Keep well-watered until plants get a good start, then water 2 or 3 times a week.*
Fertilizing Instructions: *Light mulch around each crown.*
Pruning Instructions: *Cut old stalks off as soon as flowers finish blooming.*

Other Information: Does well in full sun or partial shade. Should be divided every 3rd or 4th year.

Mrs. Harry E. Graham, Lib., Past Pres.
Terrace Tillers Garden Club
Spokane, Washington

CORAL BELLS (HEUCHERA)

Specific Variety: *Sanguinea.*
What To Plant: *Plants.*
When To Plant: *Early in spring or October.*

Daisy

Type Of Soil: *Rich, moist soil.*
How To Plant: *Plant in shallow trench, spreading out roots.*
Watering Instructions: *Water well until plants are established, then when needed.*
Fertilizing Instructions: *Humus.*
Pruning Instructions: *Cut down faded flowers from June to August so plants will rebloom.*

Other Information: A shaded, moist area is best but plants will also thrive in the sun if watered frequently. When centers become dry or dead, plants should be divided and replanted. Coral Bells make a nice airy addition to arrangements.

Mrs. Leslie Tullar
Lennox Petal Pals
Lennox, South Dakota

GLORIOSA DAISY

Specific Variety: *Single or double.*
Temperature Zone: *3.*
What To Plant: *Seeds.*
When To Plant: *Early spring or late fall.*
Type Of Soil: *Sandy loam.*
How To Plant: *Scatter seeds in shallow 1/8 to 1/4-inch trench; cover lightly. Transplant young plants, setting out 8 inches apart. Dig holes, place plants in holes. Add 1/2 cup water; let soak down. Add soil; press firmly around plant, leaving no air pockets. Press loose soil around plants; add mulch.*
Watering Instructions: *As necessary.*
Fertilizing Instructions: *Cow or sheep manure.*
Pruning Instructions: *Cut off flowers as they wither, leaving only those desired for seed.*

Other Information: Hardy in hot weather and not bothered by early frosts in spring. Plants from small to large may be moved. Plants may wilt during day but will revive during cool of evening.

Mrs. Oris Jorgensen
Irene Garden Club
Gayville, South Dakota

DAISIES

Specific Variety: *May daisies.*
Temperature Zone: *6.*
What To Plant: *Seeds.*
When To Plant: *May.*
Type Of Soil: *Well-prepared garden soil.*
How To Plant: *Sprinkle the seeds in prepared bed.*
Watering Instructions: *Keep moist until seeds germinate and are well established, then water once a week.*
Fertilizing Instructions: *Feed once lightly with 5-10-5 after plants are well established.*
Pruning Instructions: *Plants may be pruned down to ground after daisies have bloomed and their seeds have fallen.*

Other Information: Seed sown in May will bloom the following May for approximately 6 weeks. They may be planted in masses for a spectacular show. Daisies reseed themselves and never have to be planted again.

Mrs. Robert K. Fincher, Jr.
Berclair Garden Club
Memphis, Tennessee

DELPHINIUMS

Temperature Zone: *9.*
What To Plant: *Seeds or cuttings.*
When To Plant: *Fall or spring.*
Type Of Soil: *Alkaline with small amount of lime.*
How To Plant: *As soon as frost is over and soil is workable. Handle carefully so as not to break off stems coming up.*
Watering Instructions: *Keep soil moist, and protect blossoms from too much water.*
Fertilizing Instructions: *A pint of liquid plant food will help plants overcome shock of transplanting. Add 1 teaspoon of 6-6-4 to each pint of water.*
Pruning Instructions: *When cutting fresh flowers leave as much of stem as possible. When original spike has faded, cut off just below the spike, about 1/4 inch from the first leaf.*

Other Information: There are many shades of blue and other colors in delphiniums now. Originally they were of the larkspur family and were first called that but propagating and growing habits have changed that. In early times they were used for medicines or poison remedy. Also used as a remedy for body lice. In its wild species however, it ranks with locoweed in taking the highest death toll of cattle. The toxic variability extends to the point of affecting cows more readily than horses or sheep. Delphiniums grow up to 4 feet and taller and are usually blue in color.

Mrs. Ruth Newholm, Past Pres.
Glenfair Garden Club
Portland, Oregon

DELPHINIUMS

Specific Variety: *Pacific hybrids, belladonna.*
Temperature Zone: *8.*
What To Plant: *Bedding plants.*
When To Plant: *Plant in the fall after the weather gets cool.*
Type Of Soil: *Delphiniums need a rich, light alkaline soil.*
How To Plant: *Should be planted immediately, filling each hole with water and covering roots with soil.*
Watering Instructions: *Water as needed.*
Fertilizing Instructions: *Use a well-balanced commercial fertilizer in the spring, 5% nitrogen, 10% phosphate, 5% potash.*
Pruning Instructions: *Cut to ground after blooming, will often produce a second set of blossoms later in summer.*

Other Information: A 2nd feeding should be given after a 10-day rest if cut back after first bloom. It is necessary to stake the taller varieties early to prevent wind damage. If plants have all the sun, air and lime they need and are well watered when needed, they will be strong and vigorous and infection will be rare. The large Pacific Hybrids come in dark and light shades of blue, white, pink and lavender. The more delicate Belladonnas come in dark, light blue, white.

Elizabeth M. Fleming, Beautification Chm.
Lonicera Garden Club
Montgomery, Alabama

DELPHINIUMS

Specific Variety: *Pacific hybrids.*
Temperature Zone: *8.*
What To Plant: *Seeds.*
When To Plant: *Seeds planted in August or September bloom in spring.*
Type Of Soil: *Any good garden soil.*
How To Plant: *Open seed packet and add 1 tablespoon water to seeds; freeze for 1 week. Combine 1/3 part wet peat moss, 1/3 part sand and 1/3 part compost in a plastic flat. Add enough sterilized soil to*

Delphiniums

fill flat, mixing well. Sow the seeds in the flat. Cover with Kleenex; water by sprinkling the Kleenex. Store in a suitable place until the young plants have come up. Transplant in the fall. Stake the plants up; sprinkle wood ash around bases in fall and spring.*
Watering Instructions: *Water plants thoroughly once a week, being careful not to water the heads.*
Fertilizing Instructions: *Use fertilizer that is low in nitrogen on mature plants.*
Pruning Instructions: *Cut spikes down after blooming, leaving 4 leaves. Will often bloom 3 times a season.*

Mrs. Kenneth Harlow, Pres.
Juliana Garden Club
Cottage Grove, Oregon

DELPHINIUMS

Specific Variety: *Pacific hybrid.*
Temperature Zone: *2.*
What To Plant: *Seeds, hybrid plants, sport seedlings.*
When To Plant: *Spring or early summer.*
Type Of Soil: *Average garden soil.*
How To Plant: *Sow seeds in bed about 1/4 inch deep, disturbing roots as little as possible.*
Watering Instructions: *As necessary.*
Fertilizing Instructions: *A general purpose fertilizer applied in spring.*
Pruning Instructions: *Cut flower stalks off right after first blooms fade to make flowers bloom twice.*

Other Information: Delphiniums definitely are a cool climate plant. They do not do well in extremely warm or cold climates. They do not develop with full vigor if planted against a south wall where they are exposed to full sun and heat all day.

Mrs. Neil Edstrom
Top O' The World Garden Club
Gunnison, Colorado

FUCHSIA

Specific Variety: *Carmen Maria.*
Temperature Zone: *7.*
What To Plant: *Rooted cuttings started in fall from mother plant.*
When To Plant: *When weather is warm.*
Type Of Soil: *Rich porous soil.*
How To Plant: *Planter boxes or in ground.*
Watering Instructions: *Daily watering on hot days.*
Fertilizing Instructions: *Weak solution of good liquid fertilizer weekly.*
Pruning Instructions: *Prune old plants heavily. Pinch often for bushier plant.*

Other Information: Carmen Maria makes a nice bushy plant with many single light pink bells.

Mrs. Frank Johnstone
Lake Forest Park Garden Club
Seattle, Washington

HONESTY
(LUNARIA OR MONEY PLANT)

Specific Variety: *Purple or white.*
Temperature Zone: *5.*
What To Plant: *Seeds.*
When To Plant: *Early to late summer.*
Type Of Soil: *Good garden soil.*
How To Plant: *Scatter seeds on top of soil or cover lightly.*
Watering Instructions: *As needed.*

Other Information: These plants are biennials. They flower the 2nd year after sowing. Small green pods appear after flowering. Let pods grow until they become brown and plant appears to die. Test pods by rubbing between fingers. Do not pull plant until outer brown husk comes loose easily. Plants must dry in ground. Husk in garden where new plants are wanted. Dried silver pods last indefinitely. Plants like light shade.

Peggy West, W and M Chm.
Sharon Hill Garden Club
Moon Township, Pennsylvania

HONESTY
(LUNARIA BIENNIS)

Specific Variety: *Purple, pink or white.*
Temperature Zone: *5.*
What To Plant: *Seeds.*
When To Plant: *Spring.*
Type Of Soil: *Well-drained light soil.*
How To Plant: *Sow seeds between May 15 and May 30, 15 inches apart.*
Watering Instructions: *Water first few days after planting, then when necessary.*
Fertilizing Instructions: *Dried cow manure mixed into beds before planting.*

Other Information: Interesting in dried arrangements. Allow pods to dry. Remove outer layer, leaving thin transparent disk for decorative use in winter bouquets. Seed, unless sown early, will not produce seed pods until second year.

Mrs. John P. Bender, W and M Chm.
Heritage Garden Club
Mansfield, Ohio

HONESTY
(LUNARIA OR MONEY PLANT)

Specific Variety: *Purple, pink or white.*
Temperature Zone: *7.*
What To Plant: *Seeds.*
When To Plant: *Spring, summer, fall.*
Type Of Soil: *Good garden soil.*
How To Plant: *Plant in seedbeds; cover with thin layer of soil.*
Watering Instructions: *Water if leaves droop.*
Pruning Instructions: *Do not prune.*

Other Information: This plant takes 2 years to mature and reseeds itself. Grows best under drip line of trees where some sun is received. Transplant in late fall only. Remove outer layer by rubbing gently between fingers. Beautiful in dried arrangements.

Mrs. Sam W. Williams
Four Seasons Garden Club
Greenwood, Mississippi

HOSTA

Specific Variety: *Variegated.*
Temperature Zone: *9.*
What To Plant: *Plants.*
When To Plant: *Spring or fall.*
Type Of Soil: *Moist.*
How To Plant: *Not too deep in shady area 2 1/2 to 3-feet apart.*
Watering Instructions: *Water during long dry spells.*
Fertilizing Instructions: *Leaf mold and 8-8-8.*
Pruning Instructions: *Separate plants when needed.*

Other Information: Very ornamental and furnishes a beautiful border. Does well as potted plant. A friendly plant and likes to be divided. Long lived and trouble free.

Mrs. D. T. Straub, Pres.
Crestwood Circle Garden Club
Birmingham, Alabama

HOSTA

Specific Variety: *Miniature to gigantic.*
Temperature Zone: *4.*
What To Plant: *Plants.*
When To Plant: *Any time during growing season.*

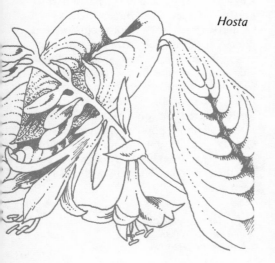

Hosta

Type Of Soil: *Loam with good drainage.*
How To Plant: *Set in bed just to the crown.*
Watering Instructions: *Water at planting, then only in extreme drought.*
Fertilizing Instructions: *A light feeding of 5-10-5 each spring.*

Other Information: I have my collection along a walk in partial shade. The plants have blooms of white or lavender lilies but I grow them for the varieties of foliage that I use in flower arranging. Chlordane dust around the plants in the spring will discourage slugs or dishes of beer set among the plants will drown slugs.

Mrs. G. L. Litzenberg, Past Pres.
Flower Arrangers Guild
Lincoln, Nebraska

HOSTA

Temperature Zone: *7.*
What To Plant: *Small plants started in containers.*
When To Plant: *March or April.*
Type Of Soil: *Garden loam or clay with bark dust and sand added.*
How To Plant: *Dig hole 3 times the size of the plant and loosen soil to a fine emulsion. Fill hole and set plant no deeper than natural dirt line. Firm soil well. Light shade is best location.*
Watering Instructions: *Never let the soil get dry.*
Fertilizing Instructions: *May use an organic fertilizer at start of growing season; needs little fertilizer.*
Pruning Instructions: *Cut off tops that die down in fall.*

Other Information: Slugs like Hostas well here in western Oregon so get slug bait out early. Hostas make delightful foliage for flower arranging; the smaller-leaved ones are best. Hostas make an excellent ground cover.

Mrs. Ed Richards, Pres.
Estacada Garden Club
Oregon City, Oregon

HOSTA

Temperature Zone: *8.*
What To Plant: *Plants.*
When To Plant: *Spring.*
Type Of Soil: *Any good garden soil.*
How To Plant: *Set in hole large enough to contain plant roots. Plants prefer shade.*
Watering Instructions: *Water when planted; water deeply when soil seems dry.*
Fertilizing Instructions: *Very little needed. Apply well-rotted manure in spring.*

Other Information: Cut off old leaves when dead. Flowers are lavender or white, leaves good to use in arrangements.

Mrs. Phil Lanning, Treas.
Lebanon Garden Club
Lebanon, Oregon

LUPINES

Specific Variety: *Russel Lupines.*
Temperature Zone: *4.*
What To Plant: *Seeds or small plants.*
When To Plant: *Late fall or early spring.*
Type Of Soil: *Does well in any soil except heavy clay.*
How To Plant: *Plant in soil 1/2 inch deep. If one color is desired, plant one seed only in each hill. If more are planted, they may be thinned.*
Watering Instructions: *Sprinkle when there is no sun.*
Fertilizing Instructions: *Fertilizing is not necessary if the plant is hearty; any fertilizer should be used sparingly.*
Pruning Instructions: *If spent blossoms are removed, smaller new ones will appear.*

Other Information: Seeds gathered in the fall should be placed in water and frozen twice in order to break the seed coating. Treat soil immediately surrounding the plant with Systemic or a similar product to combat aphids. Be careful that food products are not grown in the area.

Mrs. Mary Steadman, Hist.
Salt Lake Flower Garden Club
Draper, Utah

PENSTEMON

Specific Variety: *Various hybrids.*
What To Plant: *Seedlings or clonal material.*
When To Plant: *Late fall or early spring.*
Type Of Soil: *Low fertility, clay to sand.*
How To Plant: *Transplant seedlings, divisions and rooted cuttings.*
Watering Instructions: *Water well during establishment. Most of these plants are desert or prairie natives and dislike excessive water.*
Fertilizing Instructions: *Use little or no nitrogen. Plants do well in low fertility soils, limited moisture and full sun.*
Pruning Instructions: *Remove bloom stalks as soon as bloom is spent. Save your own seed since few seed houses offer it.*

Other Information: Seed may be obtained from the American Penstemon Society and from a limited number of dealers. Two classes are available, the large flowered tender forms derived from Mexican species and the much hardier northern forms. Leaf disease attacks the western forms in a moist climate but disease control is easy with modern fungicides. Benomyle, a new systemic fungicide is one of the best. Lygus bug, leafhoppers, thrips may cause problems unless controlled. Selected plants are easily started by division and cuttings. Many seedling populations come in a wide range of color and plant habit. Colors range from white through red, purple through blue. Recently yellows have been added.

Glenn Viehmeyer, Pres.
American Penstemon Soc.
Aching Backs Garden Club
North Platte, Nebraska

POPPIES

Temperature Zone: *7.*
When To Plant: *Spring.*
Type Of Soil: *Ordinary well-prepared soil.*
How To Plant: *According to package instructions.*
Watering Instructions: *Fine mist after sowing seed. Cover with newspaper until plants are germinated.*
Fertilizing Instructions: *Water soluable fertilizer after transplant and until well established.*
Pruning Instructions: *Cut back after flowering; clean up dead branches in early spring.*

Other Information: By planting at least one new improved perennial each year one can have a beautiful and interesting perennial border at very little cost. Plant in groups of 3 to 6 for best color effect.

Mrs. Carl Alberding, Pres.
West Union Country Garden Club
Hillsboro, Oregon

ICELAND POPPY
(PAPAVER NUDICAULE)

Specific Variety: *Yellow and orange flowering.*
Temperature Zone: *2.*
What To Plant: *Seeds or plants.*
When To Plant: *Spring.*
Type Of Soil: *Any type.*
How To Plant: *Work soil finely; sow seeds thinly.*
Watering Instructions: *Water as needed.*
Fertilizing Instructions: *Any organic or commercial fertilizer.*

Other Information: It is best to plant where flowers are to grow. Seedlings must be moved and should be established by fall in order to bloom the next summer.

Iceland poppies may be obtained in new color varieties.

Mrs. Lawrence Lillpop, Horticulture Chm.
Top Of The World Garden Club
Gunnison, Colorado

PEDILANTHUS

Temperature Zone: *10.*
What To Plant: *Cuttings.*
When To Plant: *Warm weather.*
Type Of Soil: *Good garden soil.*
How To Plant: *Full sun or partial shade. Place cuttings in small holes deep enough so plants can stand by themselves.*
Watering Instructions: *As necessary.*
Fertilizing Instructions: *6-6-6 thrown near plants in spring.*
Pruning Instructions: *Needs little pruning but may be separated for propagation.*

Other Information: Foliage is evergreen and clustered near tips of branches. Beautiful line material for flower arrangements. May be grown in garden or in urns or planter bins. Tender to cold.

Anne Gurke, Past State Pres.
Florida Federation of Garden Clubs
Hollywood, Florida

PRIMROSE

Temperature Zone: *8-10.*
What To Plant: *Bedding plants.*
When To Plant: *Spring or fall.*
Type Of Soil: *Rich garden soil.*
How To Plant: *Spread roots in hole.*
Watering Instructions: *Keep moist.*
Fertilizing Instructions: *None needed if soil is rich.*
Pruning Instructions: *Remove dead leaves.*

Other Information: Needs partial shade. Slugs love this plant.

Betty Archer
Mountlake Terrace Garden Club
Alderwood Manor, Washington

PRIMROSE (PRIMULA)

Specific Variety: *Polyanthus.*
Temperature Zone: *4.*
What To Plant: *Seedlings or plant divisions.*
When To Plant: *Early spring.*
Type Of Soil: *Well-drained, slightly acid mixture of soil and humus.*
How To Plant: *Let crown rest firmly on top of soil. Pack soil firmly around plant.*
Watering Instructions: *Water deeply, especially in hot weather.*
Fertilizing Instructions: *Compost, leaf mold or fish oil as needed.*
Pruning Instructions: *Divide plants every two to three years.*

Other Information: Pests are killed by applying Metaldehyde dust. The usual pests are root weevil and slugs. Slug bait can be placed under leaves.

Mrs. Roy McAllister, Treas.
Rainbow Gardeners
The Dalles, Oregon

PRIMROSES

Specific Variety: *Polyanthus.*
Temperature Zone: *4.*
What To Plant: *Bedding plant.*
When To Plant: *Usually early spring.*
Type Of Soil: *Sandy loam.*
How To Plant: *In good-sized hole as plant roots deep. Drainage should be good.*
Watering Instructions: *Liberal supply of water but not enough to stagnate or make ground soggy.*
Fertilizing Instructions: *Feed when green fades with fish emulsion. Avoid high nitrogen formulation.*
Pruning Instructions: *Lift and divide ungainly plants after blooming, usually 2 years.*

Other Information: Primroses can be planted in patio boxes and will take a lot of water. Red spiders attack after warm weather starts. Cut off leaves after bloom-ing; spray with malathion. Top dress with sand and sawdust. Use dieldrin in solution or dry crystals for cutworms.

Virginia Ayers, Memshp, Sunshine
Queen of Spades Garden Club
Littleton, Colorado

SHRIMP PLANT

Specific Variety: *Rose or pale green.*
Temperature Zone: *8.*
What To Plant: *Plants.*
When To Plant: *After freezes are over.*
Type Of Soil: *Slightly acid.*
How To Plant: *Set out plants as deep as original planting or plant as in pots outdoors or indoors.*
Watering Instructions: *Water holes before planting. Outdoor plants need little watering. Pot plants need weekly watering. Keep soil moist for 3 weeks until cutting develops roots.*
Fertilizing Instructions: *Top dress with barnyard fertilizer or small amount of 8-8-8 in spring and summer.*
Pruning Instructions: *Prune just below joints when plant gets too leggy.*

Other Information: Use pruned cuttings to start new plants by laying horizontally on ground and covering some of the joints with soil. May use 8-inch cuttings planting 4 inches deep in rooting bed.

Beth F. Jenkins, Alternate Fed. Dir.
Sasanqua Garden Club
Montgomery, Alabama

SULTANA OR IMPATIENS

Temperature Zone: *8.*
What To Plant: *Plants.*
When To Plant: *Early April.*
Type Of Soil: *Loamy with generous amount of humus and good drainage.*
How To Plant: *Set out in soil.*
Watering Instructions: *Requires frequent watering for good growth and blooms.*

Fertilizing Instructions: *Feed with 8-8-8 or a similar fertilizer regularly through summer.*
Pruning Instructions: *Not necessary. Plants set in ground may need size reduced when lifted in fall.*

Other Information: Not winter hardy. Must be kept inside in cold weather. Cuttings are easily rooted.

Mrs. T. Leslie Samuel, Jr., W and M Chm.
Honeysuckle Garden Club
Montgomery, Alabama

RED POKER PLANT (TRITOMA)

Specific Variety: *Red and yellow flowers.*
Temperature Zone: *8.*
What To Plant: *Rhizomes or seeds.*
When To Plant: *Spring.*
Type Of Soil: *Loose, well-drained fertile soil.*
How To Plant: *Plant 4 inches deep, 9 to 12 inches apart in sunny location.*
Watering Instructions: *Soak soil once a week in dry weather.*
Fertilizing Instructions: *Cottonseed meal, bone meal.*

Other Information: Too rich soil causes an overrampant growth. Sow the seeds in flat beds under glass in January or February. Flowering plants may be produced the same season.

Mrs. F. M. Thornton, Pres.
Spade and Hope Garden Club
Elton, Louisiana

CONFEDERATE JASMINE

Specific Variety: *Climber.*
Temperature Zone: *3.*
What To Plant: *Root of vine.*
When To Plant: *Fall or winter.*
Type Of Soil: *Well-drained light soil.*
How To Plant: *Dig hole large enough to spread roots naturally. Place vine in hole and cover with soil.*

Watering Instructions: *Water at intervals when dry.*
Fertilizing Instructions: *Fertilizer not required.*
Pruning Instructions: *Train vine on trellis or other support. Prune to desired thickness.*

Other Information: Fill hole two-thirds full of topsoil when planting; fill with water to make soil settle around the roots. Fill hole with dry soil and pack down. The small green leaves are pretty year-round.

Mrs. Lawrence B. Felder, Grounds Com. Chm.
Natchez Garden Club
Natchez, Mississippi

CLEMATIS

Specific Variety: *Jackmani.*
Temperature Zone: *4.*
What To Plant: *Pot grown specimen.*
When To Plant: *Spring.*
Type Of Soil: *Well-drained enriched soil.*
How To Plant: *Plant root ball 2 inches below surface of soil; stake up to protect. Soak soil thoroughly to settle.*
Watering Instructions: *Water thoroughly at least once each week.*
Fertilizing Instructions: *Add compost to soil in spring, a handful of 4-12-4 or equivalent. Use liquid iron if leaves are yellow.*
Pruning Instructions: *Prune back in early February to within 6 to 8 inches of soil.*

Other Information: East location is preferred. Shade root area with other plants, leaving head in the sun. Vine grows rapidly and covers trellis by May. Large purple flowers cover plant most of summer. Seed heads are useful in flower arranging. Mulch throughout the summer with light covering of grass clippings.

Mrs. Frank Wallace
Longs Peak Garden Club
Longmont, Colorado

CLEMATIS

Specific Variety: *Jackmani.*
What To Plant: *Plants.*
When To Plant: *Early spring.*
Type Of Soil: *Lime soil.*
How To Plant: *Dig a hole large enough to spread roots.*
Watering Instructions: *Water generously.*
Fertilizing Instructions: *Add generous amount of lime and dig in well.*
Pruning Instructions: *Cut off any dead branches after plant has leafed out.*

Other Information: Plant Clematis on east side of house for best results.

Mrs. Dale Henry, Pres.
Ackworth Garden Club
Indianola, Iowa

YARROW (ACHILLEA)

Specific Variety: *Plate O' Gold.*
Temperature Zone: *4.*
What To Plant: *Plants.*
When To Plant: *Spring.*
Type Of Soil: *Well-drained.*
How To Plant: *Dig shallow hole to fit roots in sunny location.*
Watering Instructions: *Water until well established.*
Fertilizing Instructions: *In spring spread 1 cup lime around each clump.*
Pruning Instructions: *Divide when plant is crowded.*

Other Information: Excellent for cut flowers. Hang upside-down and dry well for winter bouquets.

Mrs. C. J. Seidler, Pres.
Floraleers Garden Club
West Allis, Wisconsin

YARROW (ACHILLEA)

Specific Variety: *Plate O' Gold, Cerise Queen, Snowball.*
Temperature Zone: *3-4.*
What To Plant: *Root clumps.*
When To Plant: *Spring.*
Type Of Soil: *Dry, sandy, clay-type or stoney.*
How To Plant: *Clumps may be split and set 6 inches apart. Use stake supports as needed.*
Watering Instructions: *Water until established.*
Fertilizing Instructions: *Lime may be used, if desired.*
Pruning Instructions: *Cut almost to ground in fall after frost.*

Other Information: The plants have fern-like herbaceous leaves and clusters of tiny bead-like flowers from 6 inches to 2 feet tall that bloom in July and August. Pick flowers at full bloom, hang upside-down to dry for use in dry arrangements. May be spray-painted, if desired. Ageratifolia is short and may be used in rock gardens.

Mrs. Leslie Tullar
Petal Pals
Lennox, South Dakota

WALLFLOWER (CHEIRANTHUS CHEIRI)

Specific Variety: *Mixed English.*
Temperature Zone: *8.*
What To Plant: *Seeds.*
When To Plant: *July to September.*
Type Of Soil: *Sandy.*
How To Plant: *Plant in cold frame or open seedbed.*
Watering Instructions: *Keep well watered.*
Fertilizing Instructions: *Fertilize with 5-10-10 or compost.*
Pruning Instructions: *Cut back after blooming and other shoots will grow and bloom.*

Other Information: The beautiful soft colors of the English wallflowers make them wonderful bedding plants. Should be cut back to keep in good shape.

Mrs. S. H. Johnson, Master Judge
Brown's Point Garden Club
Tacoma, Washington

Bulbs

EARLY SPRING BULBS	Snowdrops Snowflakes Crocuses Squills Early Tulips	Winter Aconite Dwarf Irise Chionodoxa Early Daffodils Grape Hyacinths
SPRING BULBS	Anemones Daffodils Hyacinths Tulips Ixias	Fritillaria Late Squills Ranunculus Stars-of-Bethlehem Erythroniums
EARLY SUMMER BULBS	Alliums Caladiums Lilies Cannas Callas	Tuberous Begonias Gladiolus Tigridias Tuberoses Agapanthus
SUMMER/FALL BULBS	Dahlias Lycorises Nerines Cyclamens Colchicums	Acidantheras Haemanthus Fall Zephyranthes Sternbergias Autumn-Flowering Crocus
WINTER BULBS	Crocuses Daffodils Tulips Clivias Gloxinias	Florists' Cyclamen Tazetta Narcissus Hippeastrum Hyacinths Lilies of the Valley

ALLIUM

Specific Variety: *French Garlic.*
Temperature Zone: *7.*
What To Plant: *Bulbs.*
When To Plant: *Early fall.*
Type Of Soil: *Good garden loam.*
How To Plant: *6 inches deep.*
Watering Instructions: *Water when planted, then fall rains should give sufficient moisture.*
Fertilizing Instructions: *Very little.*

Other Information: These allium grow easily and provide ball-type flower heads to use in dried arrangements. Also used as plantings around tulip beds to discourage moles or in any area of the yard where moles are a problem. The garlic may be used in cooking and has a slightly milder flavor than the market garlic.

Mrs. Helen Morrill
Glad Hands Garden Club
Beaverton, Oregon

AMARYLLIS

Specific Variety: *Royal Dutch.*
Temperature Zone: *8.*
What To Plant: *Bulbs.*
When To Plant: *Fall.*
Type Of Soil: *Well-drained rich organic soil.*
How To Plant: *3 inches deep.*
Watering Instructions: *Bulbs in open ground need not be watered except in drought or after a feeding.*
Fertilizing Instructions: *Bone meal and cottonseed meal in fall and again in early spring.*

Other Information: Mulch bulbs in winter with grass and leaves; they will freeze in the deep south only if the winter is severe. Mulching will produce organic soil which is needed for good growth.

Mrs. F. M. Thornton, Pres.
Spade and Hope Garden Club
Elton, Louisiana

DUTCH HYBRID AMARYLLIS

Temperature Zone: *6.*
What To Plant: *Bulbs.*
When To Plant: *When outdoor weather is frost free and warm.*
Type Of Soil: *Well-drained good soil from compost pile.*
How To Plant: *Spread roots carefully and keep top of bulb above soil level.*
Watering Instructions: *Water sparingly until flower buds are well out of bulbs. Continue to water whenever necessary.*
Fertilizing Instructions: *Feed periodically with good fertilizer; water until late summer.*
Pruning Instructions: *Let plants go dry after leaves turn yellow. Cut away remaining foliage.*

Other Information: Protect from winter rains and cold with a cover of plastic. Let rest until weather is frost free and warm. Uncover and begin fertilizing and watering in about 6 weeks.

Mrs. George R. Hickey
Hoe 'N' Grow Garden Club
West Memphis, Arkansas

CALADIUMS

Temperature Zone: *8.*
What To Plant: *Tubers.*
Type Of Soil: *Porous.*
How To Plant: *Keep tubers in warm place until sprouted. Combine peat moss and sharp sand; cover tubers and keep moist. Set out in garden soil and peat moss.*
Watering Instructions: *Keep plants watered.*
Fertilizing Instructions: *Fertilize every other week with 1 teaspoon of 20-20-20 soluble fertilizer per gallon of water.*

Other Information: May plant in pots and move from place to place, if desired. Adds bright color for a shady cool spot.

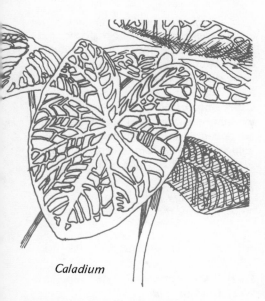

Caladium

Dig bulbs up when foliage turns yellow. Remove foliage and dust with appropriate fungicide. Store in bags or sand box until planting time.

Mrs. Berry F. Spratlan, Pres.
Annie B. Walker Garden Club
Hardaway, Alabama

FANCY LEAF CALADIUMS

Temperature Zone: *8.*
What To Plant: *Bulbs.*
When To Plant: *Late April or early May.*
Type Of Soil: *Prairie soil.*
How To Plant: *Combine soil, peat moss, sand, leaf mold and cow manure. Set out bulbs.*
Watering Instructions: *Keep moist but not soggy.*
Fertilizing Instructions: *Every two weeks with liquid fertilizer on foliage.*

Other Information: Soak bulbs overnight; warm in the oven for several hours. Store in peat moss in cabinet above oven or other warm place until sprouted.

Mrs. H. C. Horn
Ridge Acres Garden Club
Hope Hull, Alabama

CROCUSES

Specific Variety: *Dutch hybrid.*
Temperature Zone: *8.*
What To Plant: *Bulbs or corms.*
When To Plant: *Autumn.*
Type Of Soil: *Most soil conditions.*
How To Plant: *2 to 3 inches apart and about 2 inches deep. Plant along a path, on a bank, or between shrubs and beneath small trees.*
Watering Instructions: *Water only if necessary.*
Fertilizing Instructions: *No special fertilizer necessary.*
Pruning Instructions: *Allow foliage to die naturally.*

Other Information: Lift, separate and replant bulbs after foliage dies if crowded.

Mrs. Sam Roller, Past Pres.
Corvallis Garden Club
Willamette Judges Coun. Pres.
Corvallis, Oregon

CANNA

Temperature Zone: *4.*
What To Plant: *Bulbs.*
When To Plant: *Early May.*
How To Plant: *Plant bulbs in holes with eyes up. Cover with 1 inch of soil.*
Watering Instructions: *Soak thoroughly once a week.*
Fertilizing Instructions: *Barnyard manure.*

Other Information: Cut tops off within 2 inches of ground when foliage dies. Dig up clumps of roots. Wash off all soil to remove any bugs. Dry thoroughly. Place layers of newspaper in a cardboard box. Place bulbs on newspaper. Cover with additional newspaper. Close box; store in coolest part of basement.

Clara Havelka, Pres.
Wahoo Garden Club
Wahoo, Nebraska

CLIVIA

Temperature Zone: *4.*
What To Plant: *Bulbs or seeds.*
When To Plant: *Anytime for a houseplant.*
Type Of Soil: *Rich well-drained soil.*
How To Plant: *Plant bulbs in soil 1 inch below surface.*
Watering Instructions: *Keep moist until bulbs sprout and are established.*
Fertilizing Instructions: *Scott's Houseplant Food pack in spring.*

Other Information: Plant thrives on open porch in summers and blooms in early summer. Each flower sets a seed pod which matures the following summer. Remove entire flowering stalk if more flowers are wanted. No other flowers will form that year if the first flowers form seeds.

Lillian Waite
Newberry Garden Club
Newberry, Michigan

SEASONAL FLOWER BED

Specific Variety: *Tulip bulbs, poppies and marigolds.*
Temperature Zone: *6.*
What To Plant: *Bulbs, seeds, plants.*
When To Plant: *Plant tulip bulbs after frost has killed marigolds. Sow poppy seeds in January or February. Plant marigolds in June.*
Type Of Soil: *Soil, sand, peat moss.*
How To Plant: *Plant tulip bulbs according to bulb instructions. Broadcast poppy seeds, preferably on snow. Set out marigold plants.*
Watering Instructions: *Tulips and poppies are watered by rainfall. Marigolds need to be watered well once a week.*
Fertilizing Instructions: *No particular fertilizer needed for poppies and marigolds. Fertilize tulips after they have bloomed and before they are taken up.*
Pruning Instructions: *Remove tulip bulbs after foliage turns yellow. Dry and store or purchase new bulbs for the next season. After poppies have bloomed. allow them to go to seed and fall. Remove plants from bed.*

Other Information: Tulips and poppies bloom in spring. Poppies reseed themselves and never have to be resown. Marigolds bloom from summer until frost. Plant tulip bulbs for the following spring.

Mrs. Robert K. Fincher, Jr.
Berclair Garden Club
Memphis, Tennessee

DAFFODILS

Specific Variety: *King Alfred.*
What To Plant: *Bulbs.*
When To Plant: *Anytime from August until November.*
Type Of Soil: *Sandy loamy soil.*
How To Plant: *Plant bulbs about 3 inches deep.*
Watering Instructions: *Water as needed.*
Fertilizing Instructions: *Place bone meal around bulbs and work into the soil when planting. Work in bone meal again in spring.*
Pruning Instructions: *Cut leaves back after they die.*

Other Information: Be sure to let the leaves dry before cutting off or the bulbs won't flower next year.

Mrs. Odell Clary, Pres.
Bradley Rose Garden Club
Bradley, Arkansas

DAFFODILS (NARCISSUS)

Temperature Zone: *8.*
What To Plant: *Bulbs.*
When To Plant: *Fall.*
Type Of Soil: *Almost all types.*
How To Plant: *3 to 6 bulbs planted 4 inches apart and 6 inches deep.*
Watering Instructions: *Water frequently.*

Fertilizing Instructions: *Bone meal worked into soil in the bottom of holes at time of planting.*
Pruning Instructions: *Cut off old blooms. Do not cut tops. Bunch and tie for appearance.*

Other Information: Grow one color or a variety for splashes of color. Stagger groupings for a pleasing landscape design. Dust bulbs with Soildusto at time of planting. Established plantings can be treated for narcissus fly when foliage has died down. Can be removed by dusting Soildusto into foliage holes. Sand and compost worked into soil is beneficial.

Mrs. Tom Townsend
Lebanon Garden Club
Lebanon, Oregon

DAFFODILS

Specific Variety: *Trumpet.*
Temperature Zone: *8.*
What To Plant: *Bulbs.*
When To Plant: *October and November.*
Type Of Soil: *Well-drained.*
How To Plant: *Prepare soil to a depth of at least 12 inches; mix in 1/3 peat moss, compost, or rotted manure. Plant bulbs 3 to 6 inches apart.*
Watering Instructions: *Water well when planting.*
Pruning Instructions: *Pinch blooms off when dead. Foliage may be tied for neater appearance.*

Other Information: Both new and old beds of daffodils need to be fertilized twice a year. When new growth appears, make a light application of bone meal, using 1 pound per 100 square feet on new beds, 1 to 2 pounds on old beds. Make another application immediately after flowering. Plant in drifts or masses with open areas in between.

Mrs. James O. Burke, Jr., Pres.
Home and Garden Club
Lexington, North Carolina

DAFFODILS

Specific Variety: *Ceylon.*
Temperature Zone: *5.*
What To Plant: *Bulbs.*
When To Plant: *In fall before ground freezes.*
Type Of Soil: *Well-drained medium heavy loam.*
How To Plant: *Plant in bold groups in well-worked soil about 4 to 6 inches deep.*
Fertilizing Instructions: *Add bone meal to holes when planting. Mix into soil well.*

Other Information: Ceylon is a very beautiful daffodil with a smooth yellow perianth and a bright orange cup. Be sure to wait until the second year before judging its performance.

Mrs. Stanley Hepler, Idaho State Pres.
Hill and Valley Garden Club
Kendrick, Idaho

DAFFODILS

Specific Variety: *Peruvian.*
Temperature Zone: *6.*
What To Plant: *Bulbs.*
When To Plant: *When danger of frost is over.*
Type Of Soil: *Light well-balanced soil.*
How To Plant: *Well-worked soil. Plant bulbs in soil just deep enough to be supporting.*
Watering Instructions: *Very little extra watering necessary.*
Fertilizing Instructions: *Bone meal worked into soil.*

Other Information: Blooms in about 6 weeks after planting. Beautiful foliage through summer. Must be dug up before frost. Spread out to dry; store in cool place.

Mrs. C. A. Wyatt, Horticulturist
Pearl Hooper Garden Club
Memphis, Tennessee

DAFFODILS
(NARCISSUS)

Specific Variety: *Trumpet, King Alfred, Mt Hood.*
Temperature Zone: *6.*
What To Plant: *Bulbs.*
When To Plant: *Late October, early November.*
Type Of Soil: *Well-drained light soil.*
How To Plant: *Dig 6-inch holes; add 1 teaspoon of gravel or sand for drainage. Plant bulbs 8 inches apart.*
Fertilizing Instructions: *Sprinkle lightly with bone meal in the fall after 1st planting.*
Pruning Instructions: *Pinch off old heads of blooms.*

Other Information: Do not remove any leaves after blooming season. Leaves manufacture food for the bulbs. Leaves are easily raked when browned and dead. Compost beds can be covered with tree leaves in the fall and raked in spring.

Mrs. Winfred D. Polk
Four Seasons Garden Club
Corning, Arkansas

DAHLIAS

Specific Variety: *Tuberous-rooted summer and fall flowering.*

Temperature Zone: *8.*
What To Plant: *Tubers or seeds.*
When To Plant: *Spring.*
Type Of Soil: *Almost all types.*
How To Plant: *Plant 8 inches deep horizontally, eyes next to stakes. Cover with loose soil.*
Watering Instructions: *Water thoroughly early in the day to prevent mildew.*
Fertilizing Instructions: *Old manure, compost, tilled into the soil before planting, 10-20-20 sprinkled around drip line twice during growing season.*
Pruning Instructions: *Remove some buds for larger blooms.*

Other Information: Dig tubers up after frost has killed tops. Dry with cut stems down so moisture will drain out. Cut apart so an eye is on each tuber; dust cuts with sulphur, or leave in clump. Store in frost free area.

Mrs. Ray Townsend
Lebanon Garden Club
Lebanon, Oregon

DAHLIAS

Specific Variety: *All types, miniatures, BB, B and A sizes.*
Temperature Zone: *8.*
What To Plant: *Tubers with an eye showing.*
When To Plant: *May 10 through May 25.*
Type Of Soil: *Well-worked loose soil.*
How To Plant: *Plant tubers 6 to 8 inches deep with eyes up, then place stakes by each tuber carefully.*
Watering Instructions: *After plants are up and growing, water thoroughly once a week if rainfall is not adequate.*
Fertilizing Instructions: *Fertilize with Miller's Booster powder dissolved in water when plants are 6 to 12 inches high.*
Pruning Instructions: *Pinch out tips of plants for bushier plants. Disbud for show dahlias.*

Other Information: Pinch out side buds, for a better show bloom.

Mrs. Fred Spores, Awards Chm.
Eugene Garden Club
Eugene, Oregon

DAHLIAS

Specific Variety: *Hybrids.*
Temperature Zone: *8.*
What To Plant: *Tuberous roots or seeds.*
When To Plant: *Spring, in full or half sun.*
Type Of Soil: *Soil should be drained but able to hold moisture.*
How To Plant: *Place roots horizontally 6 inches deep, eyes pointing up. Mulch beds and stake.*
Watering Instructions: *Water deeply once a week.*
Fertilizing Instructions: *Bone meal, cottonseed meal. Feed during growing season and when buds appear.*
Pruning Instructions: *When 3 sets of leaves form on young plant, pinch out the center set to promote side branches. Flowers are better quality if side buds in a cluster are removed.*

Other Information: Each root must have an eye at the base of the old stem to grow. Discard all roots with no eyes. Cut off tops 6 inches above ground after first frost and burn. Let roots ripen a week, then fork them out carefully. Avoid breaking the clump from the stem. Ripen in sun 4 to 5 hours; store in cartons, tucking paper lightly over bulbs to keep out light and air.

Mrs. F. M. Thornton, Pres.
Spade and Hope Garden Club
Elton, Louisiana

DAHLIAS

Temperature Zone: *8.*
When To Plant: *Spring.*
Type Of Soil: *Deep rich soil, full of rotted manure or compost. Good drainage, plenty of moisture.*
How To Plant: *Plant in a depth of 5 to 6 inches about 24 inches apart in sunlight.*
Watering Instructions: *Keep moist; water in early morning to help prevent mildew.*
Fertilizing Instructions: *Liquid manure.*
Pruning Instructions: *Remove buds to have fewer small flowers and more large ones.*

Other Information: Dig the bulbs up when foilage dies down in the fall. Let dry; spray with insecticide. Store in a cool, dry place until next planting season.

Mrs. Herman McDuffie, Fed. Dir.
Canterbury Bells
Montgomery, Alabama

DAHLIAS

Specific Variety: *Rosea, Juarezi.*
Temperature Zone: *4.*
What To Plant: *Tubers or seeds.*
When To Plant: *May 15.*
Type Of Soil: *Any good garden soil, sunny location, good drainage.*
How To Plant: *Lay tubers flat, eyes up, in 4 to 5-inch holes. Place stakes about 1 inch from eyes.*
Watering Instructions: *Water is needed as plants grow. Water thoroughly once a week.*
Fertilizing Instructions: *Mix in bone meal at planting time. Fertilize in August with a 2-10-10 or a 4-10-5.*
Pruning Instructions: *Pinch out the top growth when plants are about 6 inches high to make plants branch.*

Other Information: In no other species of plants can one get such a large variety of colors, shapes and sizes and a blooming season from August until frost. In the colder zones the clumps of tubers must be dug and washed, being careful not to break the necks of the new tubers. Store in a root cellar or at a temperature of 40 degrees.

Mrs. Bruce H. Hull, Book Chm.
The Rainbow Gardeners
The Dalles, Oregon

DAHLIAS

Specific Variety: *Mignon mixed.*
Temperature Zone: *8.*
What To Plant: *Seeds or tubers.*
When To Plant: *Plant seeds indoors, February or March.*
Type Of Soil: *Fertile well-prepared loam in full sun.*
How To Plant: *Plant seeds in seed flats filled with vermiculite and peat. After all danger of frost is past, set plants 2-feet apart in well-prepared soil as border plants. In fall better plants will have tubers that may be saved for following year.*
Watering Instructions: *Shelter from sun and water after planting until well established root system develops.*
Fertilizing Instructions: *Compost should be dug into bed before planting. Liquid plant food added as needed.*

Other Information: Large dahlias do best if deep holes are dug and filled with crushed corn cobs to hold moisture. This must be done well in advance of planting. Soil is placed on top of the corn cobs and tubers set at proper distance from top of soil. Well-rotted and pulverized barnyard fertilizer is best fertilizer.

Mrs. J. C. Vines, Sr., Pres.
Lonicers Garden Club
Montgomery, Alabama

DAHLIAS IN ALASKA

Specific Variety: *Any of the varieties.*
Temperature Zone: *6.*
What To Plant: *Tubers.*
When To Plant: *Mid to late April.*
Type Of Soil: *Potting mix, peat moss, or vermiculite.*
How To Plant: *Start in hothouse or greenhouse a bit later than tuberous begonias are started and in the same manner.*
Watering Instructions: *Keep damp but not wet.*
Fertilizing Instructions: *No fertilizer.*

Other Information: This is a good way to insure blooming before frost in an area of short, cool summers. Transfer to beds when soil is warm enough and a good root growth has been formed.

Mrs. Al S. Wingren, Pres., Alaska Fed.
Ketchikan Garden Club
Ketchikan, Alaska

DAHLIAS

Specific Variety: *Mexican or Central American carduaceous.*
Temperature Zone: *7.*
What To Plant: *Tuberous rooted bulbs.*
When To Plant: *Spring.*
Type Of Soil: *Moderately rich soil.*
How To Plant: *Plant in sunlight.*
Watering Instructions: *Water as needed.*
Fertilizing Instructions: *Do not fertilize with nitrogen fertilizer.*
Pruning Instructions: *Pruning not usually necessary.*

Other Information: If the dahlias are to be tall, put a 6-foot stake close to the tubers when planted so as not to damage the roots later. When stalks have turned brown in the fall, dig tubers up and store in a dry cool place.

Mrs. Louie Powell, 1st VP
Whispering Pines Garden Club
Gadsden, Alabama

DAHLIAS

Specific Variety: *Cactus-style flowers.*
Temperature Zone: *5.*
What To Plant: *Tubers.*
When To Plant: *June 1.*
Type Of Soil: *Good garden soil with drainage.*
How To Plant: *Plant bulbs 4 inches deep with eyes up.*
Watering Instructions: *Water every 2 days until root system is developed.*
Fertilizing Instructions: *Superphosphate for good blooms.*
Pruning Instructions: *Removing smaller*

side buds gives larger blooms and longer stems.

Other Information: Plant dahlias as a border to screen vegetable garden. By planting in front of a split rail fence the plants may be staked securely. Bulbs must be dug up and stored in vermiculite after frost.

Mrs. Robert Mauceri, Pres.
No. Reading Garden Club
No. Reading, Massachusetts

DAY LILY
(HEMEROCALLIS)

Specific Variety: *Blended mixture.*
Temperature Zone: *6.*
What To Plant: *Herbaceous perennial bulbs.*
When To Plant: *Fall.*
Type Of Soil: *Any dry soil condition.*
How To Plant: *Set plants out with crowns of plants level with top of ground.*
Watering Instructions: *As needed.*
Fertilizing Instructions: *Rarely needs fertilizing in ordinary garden soil.*
Pruning Instructions: *May be divided after several years in early spring or after flowering.*

Other Information: Provides gardeners with a wide diversity in types in respect to habits of growth. Has no serious fungus diseases or insect pests.

Mrs. Ralph Victory, Proj. Chm.
Plain Dirt Gardeners
Newport, Arkansas

DAY LILY
(HEMEROCALLIS)

Specific Variety: *Heather Green, Charboniee*
Temperature Zone: *7.*
What To Plant: *Seeds or division of clumps.*
When To Plant: *From August to late fall.*
Type Of Soil: *Rich well-drained soil.*

How To Plant: *Requires shallow planting. Dig holes; make mounds of dirt in centers. Place plants, spreading roots. Cover with soil.*
Watering Instructions: *May be grown with very little moisture but better plants and more beautiful blooms will grow if kept moist.*
Fertilizing Instructions: *Barnyard fertilizer or commercial 10-20-10.*
Pruning Instructions: *Remove spent blooms; separate clumps when necessary.*

Other Information: More progress is being made in improving and changing the day lily. Diploid, tetraploid varieties are available. A wide range of size and color is now on the market.

Mrs. R. H. Barnes
Old Southern Garden Club
Natl. Pres., Hemerocallis Soc.
Area Accrediting Chm., Natl. Coun.
Camden, Arkansas

DAY LILY
(HERMEROCALLIS)

Specific Variety: *Blended mixture.*
What To Plant: *Tubers.*
When To Plant: *From time growth begins into autumn.*
Type Of Soil: *Any good garden soil with good drainage.*
How To Plant: *Dig holes large enough to spread out tubers; cover just above old planting line.*
Watering Instructions: *Keep moist.*
Fertilizing Instructions: *Any good flower or garden fertilizer.*
Pruning Instructions: *No pruning.*

Other Information: Do not cut the tops down in fall; leave them for mulch. Many varieties and colors ranging from pale yellow to orange and bronze. Newer varieties are showing lavender or blue colors.

Mrs. Winnie A. May, Past Pres.
Loup Valley Gardeners' Club
Callaway, Nebraska

DAY LILY
(HEMEROCALLIS)

Specific Variety: *All varieties.*
Temperature Zone: *8.*
What To Plant: *Bedding plants.*
When To Plant: *Spring.*
Type Of Soil: *Good garden loam with compost, peat and cow manure added.*
How To Plant: *Spade soil deeply and make mounds about 18 to 26 inches apart. Place plants on mounds and spread the roots. Cover so that the crown is just below the surface of the soil. Water to settle soil.*
Fertilizing Instructions: *Fertilize in the fall with 0-14-14, early spring with 8-8-8.*

Other Information: Day lilies will tolerate a lot of dry weather but should be watered during the blooming season. Plants can remain undisturbed until blooms diminish, should be dug, divided and replanted. Use force of water from the hose to help separate the entwined roots. Cut tops about 6 inches before replanting.

Mrs. W. R. McNeill
Camellia Garden Club
Montgomery, Alabama

DAY LILY
(HEMEROCALLIS)

Temperature Zone: *6.*
What To Plant: *Bulbs or roots.*
When To Plant: *April through September.*
Type Of Soil: *Light loam, peat or leaf mold added.*
How To Plant: *Shallow, 18 inches apart, well-drained area, sun or shade.*
Watering Instructions: *Plenty of water when growth is active, but does not tolerate standing water.*
Fertilizing Instructions: *First planting, rotted cow manure worked into soil, good plant food later.*
Pruning Instructions: *Leave the foliage in fall for protection against cold.*

Other Information: Peat is a good ground cover as it keeps the roots cool in summer. Watch for a fungus disease, Botrytis that attacks lilies. Rust spots or blotches on leaves or buds may be cut off. Treat cut places with a good fungicide. Dust with insecticides to control aphids or green flies.

Mrs. Edd Bussell
Frenchman Valley Garden Club
Imperial, Nebraska

DAY LILY
(HEMEROCALLIS)

Specific Variety: *Blended mixture.*
What To Plant: *Divided plants or rhizomes.*
When To Plant: *Fall or year-round.*
Type Of Soil: *Well-drained soil.*
How To Plant: *Dig holes large enough to spread roots; set crowns just level with soil.*
Watering Instructions: *Water thoroughly while blooming.*
Fertilizing Instructions: *Commercial sheep manure or cow manure.*
Pruning Instructions: *No pruning, just remove blooms.*

Lily

Other Information: Failure to bloom may be due to too much shade or plants being overcrowded and the soil exhausted. Day lilies thrive on the coast. Mulch heavily. Pine straw works well. Warm wax carefully poured into the bloom will keep a day lily open in an arrangement.

Mrs. David W. Watson, VP
Dunes Garden Club
Wrightsville Beach, North Carolina

DOG'S TOOTH VIOLET (ERYTHRONIUM)

Specific Variety: *Americanum.*
Temperature Zone: *7.*
What To Plant: *Bulbs.*
When To Plant: *Plant in fall or replant after leaves die.*
Type Of Soil: *Light soil in partial shade.*
How To Plant: *3 inches deep in masses.*
Watering Instructions: *As needed.*
Fertilizing Instructions: *Liquid fertilizer in spring.*

Other Information: Other common names are fawn or trout-lily, adders tongue. Blooms in April and May.

Sara H. Chambers, Conservation Chm.
Sussex Gardeners
Lewes, Delaware

ENGLISH WOOD HYACINTH

Temperature Zone: *8.*
What To Plant: *Bulbs.*
When To Plant: *Fall.*
Type Of Soil: *Any kind of soil.*
How To Plant: *About 3 inches deep.*
Watering Instructions: *Winter rains are sufficient.*
Fertilizing Instructions: *Bone meal, well-rotted cow manure.*
Pruning Instructions: *Thin every 3 or 4 years.*

Other Information: May be used for spring flower borders or mixed in with narcissus. None of the usual garden pests will attack these plants. Blooms every spring.

Ruby Jackson, VP
Ocean Spray Garden Club
Lincoln City, Oregon

FRITILLARIA IMPERIALIS

Specific Variety: *Crown Imperial.*
What To Plant: *Bulbs.*
When To Plant: *Fall.*
Type Of Soil: *Soil enriched with mulch.*
How To Plant: *Deep planting, wide spaced.*
Watering Instructions: *Rain and moisture of the season should be sufficient.*
Fertilizing Instructions: *Place bone meal in hole 1 inch below bulb that is planted.*

Other Information: Let foliage die after plant has produced blooms, then lift bulbs. Keep dry in peat moss until fall planting time. Will bloom year after year.

Mrs. Milton H. Wahl
Canterbury Garden Club
Wilmington, Delaware

GLADIOLI

Specific Variety: *Healthy gladioli bulbs.*
Temperature Zone: *3.*
When To Plant: *Plant bulbs early in spring when trees leaf.*
Type Of Soil: *Alkaline soil.*
How To Plant: *Dust with bulb dust to discourage thrips. Plant about 4 inches deep.*
Watering Instructions: *Keep damp.*
Fertilizing Instructions: *Superphosphate fertilizer if large quantities are planted in rows or use 4-12-4.*

Other Information: When early bulbs are blooming, plant glad bulbs. Dig glads up in fall; plant more early bulbs in same place.

Mrs. Kenneth Reilly, Bulb Timer
Cheyenne Garden Club
Cheyenne, Wyoming

GLADIOLI

Temperature Zone: *8.*
What To Plant: *Corms.*
When To Plant: *As soon as danger from frost is past.*
Type Of Soil: *Any fertile well-drained soil.*
How To Plant: *Plant the corms 4 inches deep and at least 6 inches apart in rows or in groups.*
Watering Instructions: *Soil should be given a good soaking after planting and liberal watering at intervals during dry weather.*
Fertilizing Instructions: *A generous quantity of old cow or stable manure may be mixed into subsoil. Fresh manure should not be used.*
Pruning Instructions: *Lift corms and cut off tops after flowering.*

Other Information: Cut off tops 1/2 inch above new corms. Dry in a cool frost free place. It is advisable to soak all corms in a solution of 1 gallon of water mixed with 5 teaspoons of Lysol for 1 hour. Rinse and dry. Clean off and discard the shriveled old corms and roots and store in dry conditions at about 50 degrees.

Mrs. Sam Roller, Past Pres.
Corvallis Garden Club
Willamette Judges Coun., Pres.
Corvallis, Oregon

GLADIOLI

Specific Variety: *All varieties.*
Temperature Zone: *4.*
What To Plant: *Corms.*
When To Plant: *Spring or fall.*
Type Of Soil: *Good garden soil, deeply tilled with humus.*
How To Plant: *Dig a trench in full sun 10 inches deep. Place barnyard fertilizer 1 inches deep. Place barnyard fertilizer 1 inch deep in bottom of trench. Cover fertilizer with 1-inch of soil; place corms in trench 6 inches apart. Cover with two inches of soil and continue to cover as weeding is done until corms are 6 inches*
deep in soil. This braces the tall growing floral bloom.
Watering Instructions: *Water by deep soaking.*
Fertilizing Instructions: *Glads need additional balanced fertilizer added in the watering.*

Other Information: Glad corms should be soaked in a solution of 1 tablespoon of Lysol to 1 gallon of warm water 2 hours prior to planting. Remove dried material before soaking. A series of plantings will give blooms from July to late fall. Corms to be planted late should be kept in the crisper of the refrigerator. If the corms are to be left in the ground over winter, plant 6 inches apart. Add top dressing of barnyard fertilizer 1 inch deep after the brown tops are cut. When the bed is dug, it should cure for 2 weeks after topped. Store corms in a cool dry place, using brown paper bags rather than plastic. Sprinkle napthaline flakes over the corms to control thrip. The Lysol treatment also removes this type of problem. Gladioli make beautiful cut flowers, lasting as long as 2 weeks. The spikes should be cut as for show when the first 5 blooms are open. They are beautiful in bouquets as well as in exciting special floral designs or sculpture. The color range is wider than other cut flower. Deep planting not only holds the plant upright but discourages small corms from forming.

Mrs. Tom Pethtel, Indigenous Plant Chm.
Horticultural Natl. Coun.
Plant and Pray Garden Club
Kamiah, Idaho

GLADIOLI

Specific Variety: *Various colors.*
Temperature Zone: *8.*
What To Plant: *Bulbs.*
When To Plant: *As early as January.*
Type Of Soil: *Any heavy or light soil.*
How To Plant: *Plant in sunny location, 5 inches deep and 6 inches apart.*
Watering Instructions: *Be sure to keep*

soil moist when starting to bud.
Fertilizing Instructions: *Any balanced fertilizer.*

Other Information: Cut flowers as soon as 3 or 4 florets have opened. Pull withered florets off bottom of stems and buds at top of stalk will open. Excellent cut flowers.

Mrs. Bonnie Cochran, VP
Dixie Diggers Garden Club
Montgomery, Alabama

GLADIOLI

Temperature Zone: 7.
What To Plant: *Corms.*
When To Plant: *In the spring as soon as the soil can be worked. Plant every 2 weeks until July.*
Type Of Soil: *Garden soil in full sun or very light shade.*
How To Plant: *Plant 5 to 6 inches apart and 6 to 7 inches deep in sandy soil and 4 inches deep in heavy soil.*

Watering Instructions: *Water gladioli frequently in well-drained soil.*
Fertilizing Instructions: *One or 2 side dressings with 5-10-5 fertilizer for poor soil, use sparingly when planting.*
Pruning Instructions: *Cut flowers, leaving leaves to feed the bulbs.*

Other Information: Flower spikes of most varieties should be cut after the first flowers begin to open. They will continue to open in water. Corms usually mature in about 6 weeks after blooming. Dig them before the foliage dies. The corms will rot unless dug. Dig when the soil is dry. Store in a well-ventilated dry place.

Mrs. H. T. Nesbit, Pres.
Iris Garden Club
Magnolia, Arkansas

GLADIOLI

Specific Variety: *Butterfly, Miniature.*
Temperature Zone: *4.*
What To Plant: *Bulbs.*
When To Plant: *As early as the soil is workable.*
Type Of Soil: *High in organic matter.*
How To Plant: *Soil should be spaded to a depth of about 8 to 10 inches. Plant the bulbs, right sides up.*
Watering Instructions: *A good soaking every week. Plenty of water will help more than fertilizer.*
Fertilizing Instructions: *Glads will thrive in ordinary soil but cow manure is highly recommended.*
Pruning Instructions: *No pruning is necessary.*

Other Information: When gladioli are grown as cut flowers, cutting is best done in the morning when 1 to 3 blooms are open. Leave as many leaves as possible on stems to develop new bulbs. Stems cut on a slant will take up water better.

Mrs. Palda Stagner
Community Garden Club of Alamosa
Alamosa, Colorado

GLOXINIAS

Specific Variety: *Fire King.*
Temperature Zone: *3.*
What To Plant: *Bulbs.*
When To Plant: *March.*
Type Of Soil: *Fertile.*
How To Plant: *Place bulbs on top of soil; cover with soil lightly when sprouted.*
Watering Instructions: *As needed.*
Fertilizing Instructions: *Fish emulsion after good growth is started.*

Other Information: Plants grow best in 50 to 60 percent humidity and good light. Place under Gro-Lux lamps for 16 to 18 hours a day. Plants will start to bud the last of May. Let bulbs rest when flowers fade and foliage dies. Dry the bulbs and store in a cool dry place until planting time.

Mrs. Mae Noll
Spooner Garden Club
Spooner, Wisconsin

HARDY GLOXINIA (INCARVILLEA)

Specific Variety: *Delavayi, Grandiflora.*
Temperature Zone: *8.*
What To Plant: *Plants, seeds or summer cuttings of young growth.*
When To Plant: *Early fall.*
Type Of Soil: *Rich, well-drained soil.*
How To Plant: *Plant in protected sunny location.*
Watering Instructions: *Keep soil moist. Avoid sprinkling water on flowers.*
Fertilizing Instructions: *Compost or well-rotted manure.*
Pruning Instructions: *Young growth may be pruned for rooting, under glass, in summer.*

Other Information: Incarvillea is a perennial native of China. Its five-lobed trumpet-shaped flowers are spectacular. Vivid green leaves are effective in late spring and early summer. Flowers resemble gloxinia. Winter protection is recommended.

Irene Dines Boerjan, Horticulture Study Chm.
North End Flower Club, Kennydale Garden Club
Seattle, Washington

IRIS

Specific Variety: *Bearded Iris.*
Temperature Zone: *5.*
What To Plant: *Rhizomes.*
When To Plant: *July and August.*
Type Of Soil: *Well-drained soil of moderate fertility.*
How To Plant: *Shallow planting.*
Watering Instructions: *Water sparingly.*
Fertilizing Instructions: *Spread bone meal, then use 5-15-30.*
Pruning Instructions: *Prune all dry leaves and remove all dry flowers.*

Other Information: Divide rhizomes every 3rd year and replant. For soft-rot, apply agricultural streptomiocin 1/2 teaspoon to 1 gallon water. For Iris bore, in April and May apply Sevin 1 tablespoon to 1 gallon water. For leaf spot, spray with Zineb.

Mrs. R. H. Pehle, Horticulture Chm.
Washington Garden Club
Berger, Missouri

IRIS

Specific Variety: *Reticulata, Danfordiae, Histrioides.*
Temperature Zone: *4.*
What To Plant: *Bulbs.*
When To Plant: *Fall.*
Type Of Soil: *Well-drained sandy.*
How To Plant: *3 inches deep, 4 inches apart.*
Watering Instructions: *Water when dry. Do not overwater.*
Fertilizing Instructions: *Manure or none in good garden soil.*

Other Information: The reticulata iris are the earliest to bloom in late January and

February. They make nice cut flowers and will last up to a week. The blooms are small, but make up for their size in beauty.

Mrs. William Esson, Pres.
The Rainbow Gardeners
The Dalles, Oregon

LOUISIANA IRIS

Temperature Zone: *7.*
What To Plant: *Roots.*
When To Plant: *Late summer and late fall.*
Type Of Soil: *Rich in organic matter such as manure.*
How To Plant: *Set roots 6 inches apart and 2 inches deep in damp moist soil. Irrigate heavily and mulch.*
Watering Instructions: *Frequently.*
Fertilizing Instructions: *8-8-8 as needed.*
Pruning Instructions: *Remove seed stem after flowering, unless sowing the seed.*

Iris

Other Information: Rust can damage the foliage of some species. Leaf miners can cause foliage loss in humid regions. Spray rust with Zeneb at 7 to 10-day intervals. Spray leaf miners with Cygon in fall or early spring.

Mrs. V. P. Fagan
Green Thumb Garden Club
Irving, Texas

JAPANESE IRIS

Specific Variety: *Sunset Rise, Gold Bound, Gusto, Pink Frost, Stippled Ripple, Reign of Glory, Ocean Mist, Rose Tower, Storm at Sea, Sorcerer's Triumph, Blue Pompon, Royal Robe, Queen Ann.*
Temperature Zone: *7.*
What To Plant: *Starter roots.*
When To Plant: *Early fall to October.*
Type Of Soil: *Heavily enriched; will tolerate no lime.*
How To Plant: *Plant crown about 2 inches below surface in full sun in wet spot of yard. Ideal location, along bank of stream or pond.*
Watering Instructions: *Needs an abundance of water. Water often in dry season. Plants not watered in dry season will not bloom the following year.*
Fertilizing Instructions: *Well-rotted manure.*
Pruning Instructions: *Cut off and destory tops of plants in fall after they die down so there is no protection for insects.*

Other Information: Slugs may infest iris so put bait out early in spring. These varieties are very beautiful and excellent for flower arranging. There are whites, pinks, orchids, blues, purples and combinations of colors. There are early, middle season and late bloomers. Divide when clumps get too large or they may die out. They don't like to be moved. Iris take 2 years to bloom after moving.

Mrs. Edwin Richards, Pres.
Estacada Garden Club
Oregon City, Oregon

IRIS

Specific Variety: *German.*
Temperature Zone: *6.*
What To Plant: *Rhizomes.*
When To Plant: *July to November.*
Type Of Soil: *Well-drained loam.*
How To Plant: *Place rhizomes on slightly raised mound, then spread roots evenly into the depressions. Barely cover rhizomes.*
Watering Instructions: *Water well when planting. Iris do not require too much water.*
Fertilizing Instructions: *Bone meal in superphosphate.*

Other Information: Should have not less than 6 hours sun each day. Transplant or separate every 3rd year. When planting, trim leaves in fan shapes to about 6 inches.

Mrs. C. A. Wyatt, Horticulturist
Pearl Hooper Garden Club
Memphis, Tennessee

LILIES

Specific Variety: *Olympic hybrids.*
What To Plant: *Bulbs.*
When To Plant: *Early fall.*
Type Of Soil: *Well-drained, humus-filled, friable.*
How To Plant: *Dig holes 4 to 6 inches deep, place a layer of gravel in bottom of each hole. Mix peat moss and soil; place bulbs into holes and cover.*
Watering Instructions: *Water immediately after planting, mulch well. Water in summer as lawn is watered.*
Fertilizing Instructions: *18-15-10 plus iron and sulphur, early spring top dress, keeping away from stems, smaller feedings all summer. Keep soil mulched.*

Other Information: Bulbs are never dormant. Keep ground shaded and cool with mulch or low growing annuals. Good air circulation cuts down on leaf diseases and fungus. Spray as for roses. Good drainage prevents bulb rot. Lilies may require staking. Remove faded flowers to prevent seed set which weakens bulbs. Do not remove leaves or stems as leaves are needed to increase bulb size for next year's growth.

Mrs. Glenn Viehmeyer, Horticulture Chm.
Aching Backs, Floral Doras, Platter
Planters Garden Clubs
North Platte, Nebraska

Temperature Zone: *4.*
What To Plant: *Bulbs 6 to 8 inches deep with 2 inches sand under the bulbs.*
When To Plant: *Most varieties in spring or fall. Plant Madonnas in fall.*
Type Of Soil: *Well-drained slightly acid, porous soil.*
How To Plant: *6 to 8 inches deep and 12 to 18 inches apart.*
Watering Instructions: *As needed. Bulbs will rot in poorly drained soil.*
Fertilizing Instructions: *Mulch with peat moss, bone meal and compost.*

Other Information: White, bright yellow, orange and red-pink are lovely varieties. These beautiful blooms are long-lasting and ideal for floral arrangements. They are hardy anywhere in the United States. Different varieties bloom at different times. Bulbs may be left undisturbed for years. Protect in cold states in the winter with 3 to 4 inches of straw or hay.

Mrs. Alex Rutt, Jr.
Forget-Me-Not Garden Club
Johnstown, Colorado

LILIES

Specific Variety: *Madonna.*
What To Plant: *Bulbs.*
When To Plant: *Early August or September.*
Type Of Soil: *Garden soil.*
How To Plant: *4 inches deep, 10 inches apart.*

Fertilizing Instructions: *6-8-8 in a ring 2 to 4 inches from plants.*

Other Information: Apply phosphorous every 3rd year. Plants grow 3 and 4 feet tall with 4 to 6 white blooms to the stalk. Multiplies freely. Blooms in May.

Mrs. Harry S. Wheeler
Hernando Civic Garden Club
Hernando, Mississippi

TUBEROSE

Specific Variety: *Single Mexican.*
Temperature Zone: *6.*
What To Plant: *Bulb.*
When To Plant: *After danger of frost until June 15th.*
Type Of Soil: *Good well-drained garden soil.*
How To Plant: *Cover bulbs with about 2 inches soil.*
Watering Instructions: *Same as for dahlia or gladiolus.*

Other Information: Remove bulbs before ground freezes and let dry out thoroughly. Place in plastics bags and store at 60 degrees. The most important thing to remember about tuberose bulbs is not to separate too much. Leave at least 2 good-sized bulbs and all the tiny pea-sized bulbs that will cling to the clump. Plant tuberose bulbs in the gladiolus row and dig up at the same time, leaving a lot of damp soil to dry on the clump.

Mrs. Clinton Darnell, Past Pres.
Frenchman Valley Garden Club
Imperial, Nebraska

SCILLA SIBERICA

Temperature Zone: *3-4.*
What To Plant: *Bulbs.*
When To Plant: *Early fall.*
Type Of Soil: *Sandy loam.*
How To Plant: *Set small bulbs in holes 2 to 3 inches deep, larger bulbs in holes 4 to 6 inches deep.*

Watering Instructions: *Only when planted.*

Other Information: Invaluable for planting in rock gardens, under shrubs, in wild and woodland gardens and in grassy lawns. Scatter bulbs by hand under a tree and plant where they fall. Bulbs will often be blooming before the snow is gone in the spring.

Mrs. John Groen, State Rec. Sec.
Petal Pals Garden Club
Lennox, South Dakota

FIBROUS-ROOTED WAX BEGONIAS

Specific Variety: *Semper Florens, medium red variety blooms with green leaves.*
Temperature Zone: *7.*
What To Plant: *Rooted cuttings or seeds.*
When To Plant: *April 15 or after danger of frost.*
Type Of Soil: *Slightly acid soil, north side of house or 1/2 shade.*
How To Plant: *Dig holes about 4 inches deep, insert cuttings. Cover with soil to cover roots of plant.*
Watering Instructions: *Water well when soil appears dry on top. Daily watering may be necessary in dry weather.*
Fertilizing Instructions: *Dissolve azalea food or Dawn rose food in water and sprinkle plants.*
Pruning Instructions: *Cut tall stalks to encourage new shoots at base of plants.*

Other Information: Plants may be potted in winter and grown inside in a sunny window. Seeds may be planted in January for spring planting. Height is 12 inches or less. Cuttings may be rooted in March. Small young plants are best for potting for winter because growth is small and will not get too big during winter.

Mrs. Philip C. Boyd, Treas.
Grove View Garden Club
Huntsville, Alabama

TUBEROUS BEGONIAS

Specific Variety: *Upright.*
Temperature Zone: *8.*
What To Plant: *Bulbs.*
When To Plant: *Start the bulbs indoors in February on top of bed of moist peat moss.*
Type Of Soil: *Light and fibrous, good loam, compost.*
How To Plant: *Tubers must be sprouted before placing in a flat of sand and peat moss to develop a good ball of roots. Transplant to a pot not less than 8 inches in diameter and no more than 1 inch below surface of soil.*
Watering Instructions: *Keep soil moist at all times, but never soggy. Never let plant go into night hours with water on foliage.*
Fertilizing Instructions: *Feed with fish emulsion every 10 days or 2 weeks.*
Pruning Instructions: *If the bulb has more than 1 shoot, remove one and root. Will bloom the same year.*

Other Information: Begonias should have protection from full sun and wind. Set begonias either in the pots or in the ground so that their leaves point out, never to the back of a bed. If there are few blossoms and dark green lush foliage pointing up, plants are overfeeding. Undersized blossoms with light green foliage pointing down are underfed. Should plants get mildew, spray with Karathane. Combine barnyard manure and water in a can; let stand until the color of weak tea. Makes good fertilizer.

Mabel Fabry, Past Pres.
Fir Crest Garden Club
Salem, Oregon

TULIPS

Specific Variety: *Black Tulip Early Single.*
Temperature Zone: *9.*
What To Plant: *Bulbs.*
When To Plant: *Spring.*
Type Of Soil: *Well-drained medium soil.*

How To Plant: *1 1/2 times the depth of the bulbs.*
Watering Instructions: *Do not water too often.*
Fertilizing Instructions: *Sterilized sheep manure.*

Other Information: Remove from ground after foliage begins to die. Wash and cut foliage off. Place in plastic bag and store in refrigerator until time to plant in spring.

Mrs. Victor Mather, Pres.
Hattiesburg Garden Club
Hattiesburg, Mississippi

Tulips

TULIPS

Specific Variety: *Giant trumpet, Darwin Cottage tulips.*
Temperature Zone: *8.*
What To Plant: *Bulbs.*
When To Plant: *Plant tulips in December or early January for spring blooms.*
Type Of Soil: *Porous, moderately rich soil.*
How To Plant: *Chill bulbs for a month in the refrigerator before planting. Plant 4 to 6 inches deep and about 5 or 6 inches apart.*
Watering Instructions: *Water if weather is dry.*
Fertilizing Instructions: *Mix 1 tablespoon of bone meal into the loose soil in each hole. When blooms have formed, fertilize again, working the bone meal into the soil around plants.*

Other Information: Bulbs should be lifted out of the ground every 2 or 3 years, discarding the poor bulbs. Plait the foliage when plants have finished blooming. Let foliage die down before removing. Bulbs feed on the foliage for next year's growth.

Mrs. L. B. Moon
Ridge Acres Garden Club
Montgomery, Alabama

TULIPS

Specific Variety: Darwin.
Temperature Zone: 6.
What To Plant: Bulbs.
When To Plant: October.
Type Of Soil: Fertile well-drained soil.
How To Plant: 6 inches deep in clusters.
Watering Instructions: No extra watering.
Fertilizing Instructions: Bone meal.
Pruning Instructions: Remove seed pods immediately after developing.

Other Information: Use bone meal when planting bulbs. Sprinkle regular 12-12-12 fertilizer around plants in spring when tulips first come out.

Leona Gresham, Past Pres., Parliamentarian
Fun N' Flowers Garden Club
Tullahoma, Tennessee

RANUNCULUS

Specific Variety: *Tecolote.*
What To Plant: *Bulbs or seeds.*
When To Plant: *Outdoors in spring, indoors in winter.*
Type Of Soil: *Any good soil that is well-drained.*
How To Plant: *Cover seeds with 1/4 inch of fine soil.*
Watering Instructions: *Keep moist until seeds germinate. Can be seeded outdoors in fall where climate is above freezing.*
Fertilizing Instructions: *Nitrogenous fertilizer. Lightly work around bulbs.*

Other Information: Plant in sunny location. Dig bulbs in fall and store in a cool place.

Mrs. Clarence B. Runge, Treas.
Sun Dial Garden Club
Burlington, Wisconsin

WINDFLOWER (ANEMONE)

Specific Variety: *Coronaria.*
Temperature Zone: *7.*
What To Plant: *Tuber.*
When To Plant: *October to November.*
Type Of Soil: *Rich light well-drained soil.*
How To Plant: *Soak tubers in water for 1 hour before planting. Plant 3 inches deep and 6 inches apart.*
Watering Instructions: *Keep damp during blooming season.*
Fertilizing Instructions: *Cover with leaf mold or peat moss after first frost.*

Other Information: Prefers the sun. Ideal for rock gardens, borders or pots.

Mrs. William Engelke, Pres.
Friendly Garden Club
Seattle, Washington

Roses

Growing roses is a time consuming hobby—but, there is no other plant quite like the queen of flowers. It can produce elegant blooms from early spring until frost and it offers a fantastic variety of colors, sizes, shapes and fragrances. The world's best known and most popular flower, the rose is perhaps the most rewarding of all types of garden flowers. Spectacular results can be seen within six weeks of planting and the blooms will continue for many months.

There are many types of cultivated roses—graceful hybrid tea roses, colorful floribunda roses, hardy grandiflora roses, rustic shrub roses, versatile climbing roses and dainty miniature roses. These are only the most popular categories of roses. Currently, there are more than 5,000 different varieties of cultivated commercial roses—not to mention the numerous assortment of wild roses.

Regardless of the variety of roses you select for your garden, the broad family of the genus Rosa have many of the same characteristics and can be grown in much the same manner.

All roses should be planted where they will get at least six hours of full sunshine daily. This sunny spot should also limit competition with trees and other plants for food and water. Roses do best when planted in open narrow beds. This allows air to circulate freely around the bushes lessening the danger of moldy diseases.

Since roses have no defense against excess water, rapid drainage is essential for healthy bushes. If the soil in your garden does not drain freely, it may be necessary to use a layer of cinders or pebbles at bottom of planting hole and to raise the bed three to six inches above the surrounding area.

Roses may be purchased either "bare root" or in containers. Always buy sturdy, healthy and vigorous plants from reliable dealers. Graded on a standard scale, the best roses are No. 1 and No. 1 1/2. These should have three or more canes (stalks) or canes that are 3/8 to 3/4 inches in diameter.

Rose

Fertilizing and Watering

The key to successful rose growing is to remember that the rose requires food and water both to sustain life in its existing parts and to produce new growth. The average rose bush must have thirty-five healthy leaves for each blossom, and each of these leaves must have sufficient food and water. Since most garden soils do not have enough food or moisture to feed the bush adequately, both must be added frequently.

There are special rose fertilizers on the market, but roses will do well on adequate amounts of any type of balanced fertilizer. Many rose growers apply superphosphate in the spring to strengthen the canes. High nitrogen fertilizer during the growing season will boost growth in the stem and leaf. In general, the more leaves on the rose bush, the more blossoms produced.

Most roses should be fertilized at least once a month. (Twice monthly feeding will produce the maximum number of blossoms and almost continuous blossoms.) Fertilization should be done on a regular schedule throughout the entire growing season until the end of summer. Heavy applications are needed at the beginning of the growing season and again in July.

Liquid fertilizers may be mixed according to directions in with the regular insecticide-fungicide solution. This gives a quick boost to the plant. However, the rose stops absorbing as soon as the solution dries. It is therefore wise to alternate the use of liquid fertilizer with dry fertilizer applied around the base of the bush. This gives a slower, more sustained feeding.

Roses require a large amount of water for healthy growth. But, they cannot stand "wet feet." Since roses are prone to mildew and fungus diseases, care should be taken to keep the leaves dry when watering. An exception may be made in the intense heat of midsummer when a shower will help the bushes overcome the high moisture loss through the leaves. There is less danger of disease if roses are showered in the morning so that the leaves dry before night. Weekly deep watering with a soaker hose is far better for the rose bush than frequent light watering.

Spraying

Successful rose growing depends a great deal on a regular schedule of insect and disease control. Once a pest invades the rose garden, it will be difficult and expensive to eradicate. Weekly spraying or dusting with a good insecticide-fungicide can eliminate or keep to a minimum any damage from pests.

There are several all-purpose rose dusts on the market which contain both an insecticide and a fungicide. The gardener can mix his own by using an insecticide containing lindane and malathion combined with a fungicide such as phaltan, captan, maneb or zineb.

The most successful control of rose pests demands a rigid schedule of application to prevent the pests from getting a foothold. Have a set day for spraying and *always* spray unless weather conditions prevent application. Spray or dust about once a week as soon as the first growth appears in the spring and continue until frost in the fall. During the dormant season, it helps to spray with a dormant oil to kill insect eggs.

Pruning

Roses should be pruned at the end of the dormant season. The traditional method calls for cutting the rose back to two or three feet tall (depending upon the variety) leaving only three or four of the largest canes. All pruning cuts should then be painted with a tree pruning paint to prevent insects and disease.

A rose bush is pruned each time a blossom in cut—so proper care must be taken when cutting each bloom. Always use pruners rather than scissors which can bruise the cane. Cut blooms with short stems during the spring and summer months leaving the maximum number of leaves during the growing season. The cut should be made just above a leaf containing five leaflets since the flower-producing new growth will grow from the lateral bud at this point. It is usually best to make the cut just above a leaf on the *outside* of the cane to encourage the growth in that direction.

Flower heads should be cut off just before the petals begin to fall. This will encourage new growth. In some cold climates, flowers should be allowed to seed in the late summer. This will harden the plant for the winter.

Mulch

The rose bed should be covered to the depth of two inches or more with a porous material. This will help the soil retain moisture and keep it cool during the hot summer months. The use of a good mulch will also retard weed growth.

Pine straw makes a splendid mulch where available. Cotton hulls, peanut hulls, or other loose materials are also good. Any mulch which packs (especially grass clippings) heats as it composts so lifting it once a month will help aerate the layer as well as open up drainage areas.

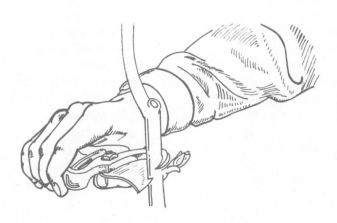

HYBRID TEA ROSES

Apollo (cream, yellow, rose)
Arlene Francis (yellow)
Bob Hope (red)
Charlotte Armstrong (red)
Chicago Peace (pink, yellow)
Christian Dior (crimson red)
Chrysler Imperial (dark red)
Confidence (pink)
Dainty Bess (pink)
Eclipse (yellow)
First Love (pink)
First Prize (pink)
Fragrant Rose (coral red)
Garden Party (ivory, red, pink)
Golden Gate (golden)
Granada (scarlet, yellow)
Helen Traubel (pink, apricot)

J. F. Kennedy (white)
King's Ransom (golden)
Medallion (apricot, pink)
Mister Lincoln (scarlet)
Mojave (burnt orange)
Oklahoma (dark red)
Pascali (creamy white)
Peace (yellow)
Pink Peace (deep pink)
Proud Land (red)
Royal Highness (soft pink)
Sterling Silver (lavender)
Summer Sunshine (golden)
Tiffany (pink)
Tropicana (orange-red)
Valencia (apricot-orange)
White Masterpiece (white)

FLORIBUNDA AND GRANDIFLORA

Angel Face (lavender)
Aperitif (yellow, pink)
Apricot Nectar (apricot)
Aquarius (pink)
Betty Prior (pink)
Buccaneer (golden)
Camelot (coral pink)
Chatter (crimson)
China Doll (pink)
Circus (yellow, pink, red)
El Capitan (scarlet)
Eutin (red)
Faberge' (pink, coral)

Fashion (coral pink)
Gene Boerner (pink)
Ginger (orange-scarlet)
Gold Cup (golden)
Golden Slippers (golden)
John S. Armstrong (deep red)
Montezuma (orange)
Ole' (scarlet
Queen Elizabeth (rose pink)
Redgold (yellow with red edges)
Saratoga (white)
Spanish Sun (yellow)
Spartan (orange-red)

CLIMBING ROSES

American Pillar (red)
Blaze (scarlet)
Coral Dawn (coral pink)
Crimson Glory (red)
Don Juan (velvet red)
Golden Showers (yellow)
Hollande (dark crimson)

Mermaid (yellow)
New Dawn (pink)
Parade (red)
Paul's Lemon Pillar (lemon white)
Radiance (red)
Royal Gold (yellow)
White Dawn (white)

MINIATURE ROSES

Baby Betsy McCall (pink)
Baby Masquerade (red)
Cinderella (white)
Dwarfking (red)
Red Imp (deep crimson)

Robin (red)
Scarlet Gem (orange-scarlet)
Sweet Fairy (pink)
Tinker Bell (pink)
Twinkles (white)

No matter which type rose you select to grow, there are a few basic rules that should be followed:

1. Purchase only healthy rose bushes from a reputable garden shop, local nursery, mail-order nursery or retail store.
2. Plant immediately. Do not let the roots dry out or be exposed to the sun.
3. Select a site that will receive at least six hours of sunshine each day.
4. Place plants in a well-prepared bed.
5. Keep the plants well watered.
6. To prevent insect and disease damage, dust or spray often.
7. To keep plants healthy and well groomed, prune each year.

GENERAL INSTRUCTIONS
FOR GROWING ROSES

Temperature Zone: *6.*
What To Plant: *Bushes.*
When To Plant: *Spring.*
Type Of Soil: *Well-prepared, well-drained beds.*
How To Plant: *Dig large deep holes. Mix in gypsum, bone meal, limestone and German peat. Place bushes in holes, spreading roots evenly. Plant bushes with bud unions level with soil.*
Watering Instructions: *Water generously in the morning.*
Fertilizing Instructions: *Any good rose fertilizer applied as directed.*
Pruning Instructions: *Always leave at least one set of leaves with five leaflets for another rose to appear when cutting roses.*

Other Information: Overhead watering may be done in the morning, but spray after 5 o'clock. Spraying with proper insecticides and fungicides will control bugs, mildew and black spot. Regular spraying is necessary at least once a week in the spring and every 10 days in summer. Always spray undersides of leaves as well as tops.

Mrs. J. George Hettiger, Past Pres.
Rambler Garden Club
Louisville Rose Society
Coun. of Federated Garden Clubs
Louisville Area
Jeffersontown, Kentucky

GENERAL INSTRUCTIONS
FOR GROWING ROSES

Temperature Zone: *4.*
What To Plant: *1 to 2-year old shrubs.*
When To Plant: *April or May.*
Type Of Soil: *Heavy well-mixed soil mixed with peat moss.*
How To Plant: *Dig holes 14 inches wide and 1 foot deep. Plant roses so roots will assure natural position.*
Watering Instructions: *Water well when*

planting; tamp soil to remove air pockets. Water once a week thereafter.
Fertilizing Instructions: *Fertilize when plants are in full leaf and after first blooms.*
Pruning Instructions: *Prune to 10 to 12 inches. Cut stems to 8 inches from ground.*

Other Information: Mound roses 8 to 10 inches above ground with good soil for winter protection. Remove soil gradually when buds begin to swell.

Elisa K. Schaak, Pres.
Community Garden Club of Alamosa
Alamosa, Colorado

APHID CONTROL

Combine 1 cup of finely chopped green onions and 1 quart of water; soak overnight. Drain. Spray onion water on any plants affected by aphids. Repeat as often as necessary.

Mrs. Cleve Allen, Jr., Pres.
The Garden Clubs of Mississippi, Inc.
Gulfport, Mississippi

GENERAL INSTRUCTIONS
FOR GROWING ROSES

Temperature Zone: *6.*
What To Plant: *Bushes.*
When To Plant: *About March 20th.*
Type Of Soil: *Any good soil.*
How To Plant: *Dig deep wide holes. Fill each hole with water and 1 tablespoon fish fertilizer. Mound soil in bottom of holes; place plants on mounds, roots down. Combine topsoil and wet peat moss; cover roots with mixture, watering well.*
Watering Instructions: *Place hose on ground near plants. Water to a depth of 14 inches once a week. Water frequently in hot weather.*
Fertilizing Instructions: *Mag Amp may be used as a slow release fertilizer. Dig rings around plants 2 to 3 inches deep and 10*

inches from stems. Fill each ring with 1 cup liquid fertilizer.

Pruning Instructions: *Prune bushes 6 to 8 inches in height for exhibition blooms. Prune 14 inches in height, leaving 3 to 5 strong canes, for numerous blooms. Cut at a 45 degree angle 1/4 inch above outside eyes. Seal canes. Old roses should be pruned after the first bloom. Cut out dead wood.*

Other Information: Feed roses at pruning time and after heavy June and late July blooms. Spray with Isotox for worms and thrip, Acti-dione for mildew.

Ann Kachinsky, Rose Judge
Growing Pains Garden Club
Spokane, Washington

PROPAGATION BY SOFTWOOD

Specific Variety: *All varieties.*
Temperature Zone: *8.*
What To Plant: *Cuttings.*
When To Plant: *When bloom fades.*
Type Of Soil: *Sharp sand.*
How To Plant: *Cut blooming stem on slant below node of second set of 5 leaves. Remove blossom, bottom leaf and all but 2 leaves of each leaf cluster. Dip roots into Rootone; insert cuttings in sharp sand in pots to depth just below first cluster.*
Watering Instructions: *Keep moist.*
Fertilizing Instructions: *Fertilize with balanced fertilizer according to package instructions at 2-week intervals after potting.*

Other Information: Keep in shady location. Repot in potting soil in 1 part each garden loam, peat moss and sand. When cutting grows a 6-inch top, keep in shade a few days. Remove to full sun. Keep pots in cold frame first winter. Plant in garden in late March or April.

Mrs. Fred B. Davis, Pres.
Stoneville Garden Club
Stoneville, North Carolina

GENERAL INSTRUCTIONS FOR GROWING ROSES

Temperature Zone: *5.*
What To Plant: *Bushes.*
When To Plant: *Spring.*
Type Of Soil: *Good garden soil.*
How To Plant: *Dig holes large enough to spread out roots. Space plants for good circulation.*
Watering Instructions: *Keep ground moist but not soggy. Do not water late in the day.*
Fertilizing Instructions: *Good balanced fertilizer early in spring and at blooming time and late summer.*
Pruning Instructions: *Remove all diseased wood; eliminate stems crossing. Cut above eye, choosing ones that point in desired direction. Cut out all tiny cones, leaving 5 or 6 heavy cones about 12 inches tall.*

Other Information: Burn all fallen leaves that have been attacked with black spot, mildew and rust. Spray for sucking and chewing insects, spraying well on top and underneath. Plant chives or garlic in an inconspicuous spot in the rose bed.

Mrs. W. L. Weber
Lincoln Heights Garden Club
Spokane, Washington

GENERAL INSTRUCTIONS FOR GROWING ROSES

Temperature Zone: *8.*
What To Plant: *Bushes.*
When To Plant: *February.*
Type Of Soil: *Well-drained garden soil.*
How To Plant: *Dig deep holes; plant bushes at same level as grown in pots, spreading roots evenly.*
Watering Instructions: *Water thoroughly every morning during dry spells. Do not water foliage.*
Fertilizing Instructions: *Combine rose plant food and sheep fertilizer in planting soil. Feed throughout season.*
Pruning Instructions: *Prune back to about 6 inches when planted. Keep roses cut every day when in bloom.*

Other Information: Plant chives and garlic among bushes to prevent insects. Mulch bed 6 inches deep using old hay to hold moisture.

Mrs. D. L. Booger
Anniston Garden Club
Anniston, Alabama

ROSE CUTTINGS

Specific Variety: *Cuttings of any variety.*
Temperature Zone: *6.*
What To Plant: *About 6 inches of hardened branch, preferably with a joint.*
When To Plant: *September through November.*
Type Of Soil: *Sandy, well-drained.*
How To Plant: *Cut small white potatoes and insert the rose cuttings; plant in fall. Cover with glass jars; leave until warm weather.*
Watering Instructions: *The potato takes care of the watering needs for the dry fall months.*

Other Information: Do not leave glass jars over plants during the day after the leaves come out in spring and the sun is quite warm. Remove jars in day time; place back on at night until weather is quite warm.

Mrs. Ovel Shelton, Pres.
Garden Gate Garden Club
Dickson, Tennessee

ROSE CUTTINGS

When To Plant: *September to May outdoors, May to September indoors.*
Type Of Soil: *Sand or vermiculite and peat moss.*
How To Plant: *Cut blooms off; trim leaflets, leaving only 3 on a leaf stem. Cut ends with sharp knife diagonally.*
Watering Instructions: *Keep moist but not wet.*
Fertilizing Instructions: *Dust with all-purpose rose dust for mildew and black spot.*

Other Information: Plant prepared rose cuttings in outdoor soil; cover with tall fruit jars. Keep out of direct sun if weather is very warm. May transplant when plants are well established.

Dr. Gilbort D. Jay, III, Judge Consultant
Memphis Rose Society of Tennessee
West Memphis, Arkansas

GARDEN PARTY

Temperature Zone: *8.*
What To Plant: *Plants.*
When To Plant: *Late fall.*
Type Of Soil: *Mix 1/2 garden soil, 1/4 peat moss and 1/4 sand; add well-rotted manure.*
How To Plant: *If soil is alkaline, dig down 24 inches and pile soil above ground for drainage.*
Watering Instructions: *Soak thoroughly once a week. Do not wet foliage.*
Fertilizing Instructions: *Apply fertilizer with a ratio of 1-2-1 when growth begins. Continue monthly.*
Pruning Instructions: *Cut back in February to 3 strong 8-inch outside stalks.*

Other Information: *Spray weekly for aphids and fungus.*

Mrs. Ed Rankin, Treas.
Ridge Acres Garden Club
Montgomery, Alabama

CHARLOTTE ARMSTRONG

What To Plant: *Plants.*
When To Plant: *Winter, when bushes are dormant.*
Type Of Soil: *Any good garden soil.*
How To Plant: *Dig a 12 x 18-inch hole 12 inches deep to hold plant.*
Watering Instructions: *Water well when planted; water frequently, soaking soil to a depth of 8 to 10 inches at base of plant.*
Fertilizing Instructions: *Roses grow best in slightly acid soil, use complete fertilizer such as 5-10-5, 4-8-4 or 4-8-6.*
Pruning Instructions: *Prune annually; cut away dead growth using a sharp tool. Make all cuts to canes where buds face outward.*

Other Information: Buy roses from reputable local nursery. Never buy roses with waxed stems or bare roots. Plants should have at least 6 hours of sun, if possible. Spray or dust regularly to prevent insects or disease damage. Plant roses at least 3 feet apart.

Mrs. W. W. Watson
Clayton Garden Club
Clayton, Alabama

FIRST LOVE

What To Plant: *Rose bush.*
When To Plant: *March 1st.*
Type Of Soil: *Sandy loam or clay soil.*
How To Plant: *Dig a large hole for each plant. Place the plants in the holes to the depth of the graft, spreading the roots out well. Cover the roots with half of the loose soil; fill holes with water. Spread the remaining soil around the plants.*
Watering Instructions: *Water once a week during dry season.*

Fertilizing Instructions: *Fertilize June 1st.*
Pruning Instructions: *Prune plants on March 1st.*

Other Information: Combine liquid fungicide and insect spray; spray plants well.

Mrs. Harry A. Graham, Pres.
Coahoma Woman's Club, Garden Div.
Coahoma, Mississippi

HELEN TRAUBEL

What To Plant: *Shrub.*
When To Plant: *February.*
Type Of Soil: *Light loam.*
How To Plant: *Dig a 2-foot hole, mixing the soil loosely. Place the plant in the hole to the depth of the bud union. Replace the soil around the plant.*
Watering Instructions: *Once a week.*
Fertilizing Instructions: *Once a month using 14-0-14.*
Pruning Instructions: *Light pruning in fall, heavy in spring.*

Other Information: Spray the plant regularly for pests and fungus.

W. A. Salter
Birmingham Rose Soc.
Birmingham, Alabama

FIRST PRIZE

What To Plant: *Rose bushes.*
When To Plant: *February 1st to 15th.*
Type Of Soil: *Good or normal garden soil.*
How To Plant: *Dig a hole for each plant wide and deep enough to accomodate roots when spread out. Pile a cone of soil in bottom of hole so that crown of plant may seat firmly with roots fanning outward. After seating the plant, hold it level and work loose top soil and humus over and under the roots so there will be no air pockets. Fill the hole three-quarters full of water and allow water to settle. Leave the bud joint just above the ground. Mulch plants well.*
Watering Instructions: *Water plants twice a week in summer.*
Fertilizing Instructions: *Do not fertilize plants until they are growing well.*
Pruning Instructions: *Prune to desired height on March 15th, removing all dead wood and inside limbs that are weak.*

Other Information: Give plants loving attention and water frequently.

Mrs. Robert L. Cottle, Sec.
Petal Lovers Garden Club
Tallassee, Alabama

NEW YORKER

Temperature Zone: *3.*
What To Plant: *Bushes.*
When To Plant: *Late May.*
Type Of Soil: *Heavy dark mountain soil.*
How To Plant: *Loosen the soil; add fertilizer, mixing well. Blow the soil containing straw and other light materials. Dig large holes; water well. Plant bushes firmly.*
Watering Instructions: *Water well when planting, then water as needed.*
Fertilizing Instructions: *Ortho or well-rotted barn manure.*
Pruning Instructions: *Early spring.*

Mrs. L. R. Swan
Rainbow Garden Club
Great Falls, Montana

MEDALLION

Temperature Zone: *10.*
What To Plant: *Plants.*
When To Plant: *Mid March.*
Type Of Soil: *Well-drained with good humus.*
How To Plant: *Dig large enough holes to allow good root growth. Plant with roots spread over mounds and bud unions at ground level.*
Watering Instructions: *Weekly soaking.*
Fertilizing Instructions: *Bone meal in fall and spring. All-purpose fertilizer or Alaska fish fertilizer occasionally.*
Pruning Instructions: *Prune tip growth only in fall. Hard prune by March 15 to 3 outstanding thick branches.*

Other Information: Do not use chemical sprays on roses. Plant 3 onion sets below each rose bush to prevent insects or disease. Plants are strong and have good resistance.

Agnes Kangas
Dirt Dobbers Garden Club
Shelton, Washington

PEACE

Temperature Zone: *3.*
What To Plant: *Plants.*
When To Plant: *April or middle May.*
Type Of Soil: *Sandy loam.*
How To Plant: *Plant roses about 2 inches above grafts in deep holes. Water generously to straighten roots. Press soil firmly around plants.*
Fertilizing Instructions: *Compost weekly or as much as needed for growth.*
Pruning Instructions: *Prune only for the winter kill in spring.*

Other Information: Roses do very well in summer and produce a lot of blooms. Spray with liquid soap solution and Ortho for insect damage.

Mrs. Perry Oakley, VP
Big Sky Garden Club
Superior, Montana

PEACE

Temperature Zone: *4.*
What To Plant: *Plants.*
When To Plant: *Spring.*
Type Of Soil: *Good dark fertile soil.*
How To Plant: *Plant in large deep holes for roots to extend.*
Watering Instructions: *Water to soak the soil when planting. Water at least twice a week during summer.*
Fertilizing Instructions: *About once a month with rose food fertilizer.*
Pruning Instructions: *Prune in spring, cutting off all dead parts. Prune part way down in late fall.*

Other Information: Roses must be dusted frequently for insects and mildew. Cut off all dry flowers and roses to continue setting on buds if weather is not too hot. The peace rose is a large yellow solid flower with a pink edge and shiny green leaves.

Mrs. Otto Hamann, VP
Leigh Garden Club
Leigh, Nebraska

HYBRID TEAS

What To Plant: *2-year old field grown bushes with canes grafted onto vigorous understock.*
When To Plant: *Last week in February or 1st week in March.*
Type Of Soil: *Well-drained, mulchy soil with PH 6.5 to 6.8.*
How To Plant: *Dig tub-sized holes 1 1/2 feet deep in area that gets 1/2 day sunshine. Shape mounds in the bottom of each hole. Soak roots of plants in water; plant bushes with bud unions on top of soil. Fill in with soil, packing tightly. Water well. Place baskets over bushes for 2 weeks.*
Watering Instructions: *Water plants well before weekly spraying. Water every 3 days thereafter.*
Fertilizing Instructions: *1 cup balanced rose food every 2 weeks. Add trace elements according to package instructions. Feed each bush with 1/2 cup Epsom salts in spring.*
Pruning Instructions: *Cut bushes back to about 1 1/2 feet from ground the 1st of March. Do not cut Peace variety back as much. Wind tops in December, cutting off any diseased wood.*

Other Information: Roses must be sprayed once a week for prevention of diseases and insect damage. Spray with Benlate to prevent mildew. Spray with Acti-Dione PM for black spot. Keep all diseased leaves picked off between sprayings. Spray with Isotox to prevent insects.

Mrs. Gerald K. Daniel
Am. Rose Society Accredited Judge
Consulting Rosarian
Oak and Elem Garden Club
Memphis, Tennessee

SUB-ZERO, HYBRID TEA

What To Plant: *Plants.*
When To Plant: *Spring.*
Type Of Soil: *Light.*
How To Plant: *Dig a 2-foot hole for each plant. Place leaves, rotted manure and bone meal in each hole. Plant the roses, leaving a trench around each bush for watering.*
Fertilizing Instructions: *Fertilize plants with Ra-Pid-Gro every 2 weeks until August 1st.*
Pruning Instructions: *Prune the roses on the last of April or early in May.*

Other Information: Place crushed egg shells around roses to repel bugs and Japanese beetles. Egg shells add lime to the soil. Protect the roses from cold weather by placing 9-inch collars filled with soil around the roses. Spread leaves over the soil.

Jean Randall
Springfield Garden Club
Springfield, Vermont

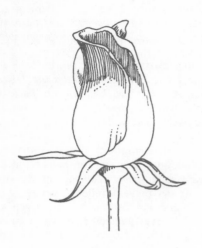

PINK CUSHION ROSE

Temperature Zone: *3.*
When To Plant: *Spring.*
Type Of Soil: *Sandy loam mixed with compost.*
How To Plant: *12 to 14 inches deep.*
Fertilizing Instructions: *Fertilize with 5-10-5 in May and August. Feed in October with bone meal.*
Pruning Instructions: *Cut to 4 strong 10-inch high stems in spring.*

Other Information: Blooms the first year from July to end of October. Available through Sterns Nurseries, Seneca, New York 14456.

Mrs. Joseph Klauser, Hosp. Chm.
Lake George Garden Club
Lake George, New York

HYBRID TEA

Temperature Zone: *8.*
What To Plant: *Hybrid teas, floribundas, grandifloras.*
When To Plant: *December 15 thru February.*
Type Of Soil: *Well-drained average soil.*
How To Plant: *Plant the roses in large holes, mounding the soil under each plant and spreading the roots out. Plant roses with graft even with ground. Mulch the roses; remove mulch early in spring.*
Watering Instructions: *Water the roots as overhead sprinkling is not too satisfactory. Water before extreme heat of day.*
Fertilizing Instructions: *Fertilize the plants when 2 leaves have appeared on each plant. Fertilize on March 15th using 6-10-4. Fertilize again in July using 5-10-5.*
Pruning Instructions: *Prune the plants the last week in February or March 1st. Prune to the outside bud so air can circulate in center of plant. Cut out all dead or crossed stalks, cutting to desired height. Cut to an inside eye, leaving 3 to 5 canes. Leave cuts open for 24 hours. Paint cuts with tree sealer. Do not cut below a 5 leaflet when cutting roses to prevent candelabras.*

Mrs. R. R. Troxel, Pres.
Fir Crest Garden Club
Salem, Oregon

HYBRID TEAS

Temperature Zone: *7.*
What To Plant: *2-year old plants.*
When To Plant: *March 15.*
Type Of Soil: *Slightly acid.*
How To Plant: *Dig holes 12 inches deep; fill with peat moss and cow manure. Set plants on mounds and cover.*
Watering Instructions: *Soak soil when planting. Water again in 2 or 3 days. Water every 2 or 3 days all summer.*
Fertilizing Instructions: *Cover grafts with 2 or 3 inches of manure in spring. Apply Dawn rose food according to directions.*
Pruning Instructions: *Prune March 1st.*

Other Information: Spray weekly and after rains. Use Phalton for black spot, Malathion for insects and Acti-dione PM for mildew.

Mrs. Philip C. Boyd, Treas.
Grove View Garden Club
Huntsville, Alabama

ROYAL HIGHNESS

When To Plant: *October or November.*
Type Of Soil: *Well-drained heavy loam.*
How To Plant: *Prepare rose bed several weeks before planting. Dig a hole 20 to 24 inches deep and 16 to 18 inches across for each plant. Work compost or other organic materials into subsoil, mixing well. Work leaf mold and peat moss into the upper soil, mixing well. Pack soil under roots down well, then set bush into prepared soil, being sure the roots will not come in contact with the organic mixture and get burned. Set the bush so that the graft or bud union is just below the ground. Spread out roots carefully, then fill in with fertile top soil. Pack down soil with a stout stick 3 or 4 inches. Fill with water 2 or 3 times and let water drain away. Finish filling hole with soil and mulch with straw, leaves or peat moss.*
Watering Instructions: *Soak ground down to 8 or 9 inches every 4 or 5 days during dry weather.*
Fertilizing Instructions: *1/2 cup rose food for each bush.*
Pruning Instructions: *Cut back in February to 2 or 3 canes 16 to 18 inches high with bud on outside.*

Other Information: Roses may be fertilized with liquid fertilizer. Bushes must be sprayed with prepared sprays or dusted with rose dust for insects and black spot.

Effie C. Haber, Telephone Com.
Woodhaven Garden Club
Montgomery, Alabama

HYBRID TEAS

What To Plant: *Plants.*
When To Plant: *2nd week in March.*
Type Of Soil: *2/3 garden soil, 1/3 peat moss.*
How To Plant: *Dig 18 x 24-inch holes; fill hole 2/3 full of water, then drain. Plant roses.*
Watering Instructions: *Keep well watered.*
Fertilizing Instructions: *5-10-5 applied first of April, May, June and July.*
Pruning Instructions: *Prune slightly after 1st freeze; prune again in spring.*

Other Information: Spray for black spot weekly or after a rain using Phalton.

Mrs. Seth Cooper
Mt. Pleasant Garden Club
Mt. Pleasant, Tennessee

EUTIN FLORIBUNDA

Temperature Zone: *3.*
What To Plant: *Selected 2 year No. 1 bushes.*
When To Plant: *Early spring.*
Type Of Soil: *Good garden soil.*
How To Plant: *Dig a large hole, then make a mound in center to support bush. Place on mound, spreading roots downward carefully. Place soil over roots and tamp down firmly. Water well to settle soil, then fill again, as needed.*
Watering Instructions: *Water well in dry weather. Soak ground; do not sprinkle over bushes.*
Fertilizing Instructions: *2 applications rose fertilizer in spring and another in late summer. Do not fertilize in fall.*
Pruning Instructions: *Remove faded flowers. Cut blooms back to 5 leaf clusters.*

Other Information: Cut tops back to 6 inches at planting time. Mound with soil and let remain for a week to 10 days. Remove soil slowly and carefully. To protect bushes, cover with lots of leaves in fall, then cover leaves with wood or other material to keep leaves in place. Remove around middle of April and cut tops back to 6 inches.

Mrs. Hjalmer Nelson
Bancroft Garden Club
Bancroft, Nebraska

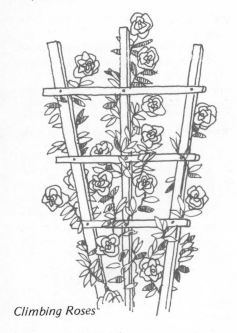

Climbing Roses

BUCCANEER GRANDIFLORA

Temperature Zone: *9.*
What To Plant: *Bush.*
When To Plant: *October.*
Type Of Soil: *Well-drained.*
How To Plant: *18 inches deep in large hole.*
Watering Instructions: *Water well 3 times a week.*
Fertilizing Instructions: *Ammonium phosphate and blood meal in fall; cover with peat moss.*
Pruning Instructions: *January 29th prune older plants to 3 feet, smaller plants to 2 feet in height.*

Other Information: Plant 6 onion sets around each bush. Keep soil loose.

Mrs. Clokey Moore, Pres.
Los Palos Verdes Garden Club
Tucson, Arizona

MINIATURE ROSE

Specific Variety: *Frosty.*
Temperature Zone: *7.*

What To Plant: *Young potted plants.*
When To Plant: *Late March or early April.*
Type Of Soil: *Clayey loam.*
How To Plant: *Loosen soil thoroughly. Spread roots carefully, then set plants in soil a little deeper than planted in pot.*
Watering Instructions: *Water well at planting, then finish filling in soil and firm down. Water as needed in dry weather.*
Fertilizing Instructions: *Use bone meal before planting, then feed with any rose fertilizer.*
Pruning Instructions: *Prune back to about 2 inches from ground about middle of March.*

Other Information: Frosty grows to 6 inches high with a 12-inch spread. Foliage is very glossy and does not mildew. The flowers are double, fragrant, very white and about 1 1/4 inches across when fully open. The plant is hardy and blooms heavily through a long season. Fine as a border.

Genevieve Stivers, VP
Lake Forest Park Garden Club
Seattle, Washington

MINIATURE ROSE

Specific Variety: *Cri Cri.*
Temperature Zone: *6.*
What To Plant: *Plants.*
When To Plant: *Anytime.*
Type Of Soil: *Sterilized potting soil.*
How To Plant: *In container 6 to 8 inches in diameter with pebbles covering drainage holes.*
Watering Instructions: *Only when soil feels dry to the touch.*
Fertilizing Instructions: *Every 2 weeks, using liquid houseplant fertilizer.*
Pruning Instructions: *Prune plant to conform to size of container.*

Other Information: Grown indoors under fluorescent light, brought to flower and moved to display area until flowers fade, then returned to light to promote new growth and flowering will make interesting and different houseplants.

Mrs. James Vincent, Pres.
Henderson Co. Garden Club
Robards, Kentucky

CLIMBING ROSE

Specific Variety: *Blaze.*
Temperature Zone: *4.*
What To Plant: *Moss-protected, No. 1 grade green-caned bush.*
When To Plant: *Early in spring as possible.*
Type Of Soil: *Well-drained soil.*
How To Plant: *Provide trellis or preferably a fence. Tie canes to supportive structure in the early growing years. Prepare a bed in an airy place. Cultivate soil 18 inches deep with manure or a handful each of peat moss, dricanure and milorganite. Soak roots in a pail of water or mud overnight before planting. Trim off small weak broken twigs and roots. Trim to about 13 inches high. Dig holes at least 12 inches deep and 18 inches wide. Make mounds of loose soil in middle of holes; spread roots over mounds. Set graft at ground level. Fill some dirt in around roots carefully. Firm and soak with water. Fill in dirt up to graft; soak again. Pull soil up around plants about 9 inches and leave for a day or two until the weather warms up and the plant is used to the outdoors. Pull dirt away gradually. Firm soil around plant just below graft.*
Watering Instructions: *Water deeply when soil is dry. Do not get water on leaves if possible. Water in the morning.*
Fertilizing Instructions: *Complete plant food or rose food. Feed new bushes after first crop of blooms and then after each crop of blooms. Feed old bushes when pruning and again after each bloom. Stop feeding in August so new canes will not freeze.*
Pruning Instructions: *Clip out all dead and diseased wood. Take out an old cane once in a while from an older bush to*

encourage a new cane to grow. Cut back all stems on all canes to within 3 inches of canes to encourage mass blooms on climbers. Climbers bloom only on old canes so new ones will just need to be positioned.

Other Information: Climbers need winter protection, so bring in from another place a bucket of soil to cover the roots. A really bad climber situation can be rectified by cutting the whole bush down to within 6 inches of the ground and letting it start a new life. Climbers are less subject to pests than tea roses but still need to be watched and protected from aphids and blackspot. Cutting off faded blooms does encourage growth elsewhere and improves the appearance of the climber.

Mrs. Robert C. Graham, Horticulturist
Ann Arbor Garden Club
Ann Arbor, Michigan

CLIMBING ROSES

Specific Variety: *Seven Sisters.*
Temperature Zone: *7.*
What To Plant: *Rooted bushes.*
When To Plant: *Spring.*
Type Of Soil: *Acid.*
How To Plant: *Plant bushes next to a fence. Mix soil with peat moss and gravel. Pat soil up around fork of roots.*
Watering Instructions: *Water only when there is a dry spell.*
Fertilizing Instructions: *Any available manure in the spring and fall. Add pine needles.*
Pruning Instructions: *Cut back severely to the top of the fence in late summer and fall.*

Other Information: Good plants for drying and making miniature picture arrangements. Cut branches when buds have just formed; place in attic. Buds hold their color very well.

Mrs. Sam Skipper, Pres.
Crestwood Garden Club
Chattanooga, Tennessee

Shrubs

Sturdy, long-lived shrubs usually are considered the backbone of any landscape plan developed for the home grounds. Being more or less permanent, often large and varying in colors and textures they provide the home with year-round beauty and interest.

Flowering shrubs are available in many sizes and shapes—from slow growing compact miniatures to fast growing large open branched specimens in an array of colors—bright red, pale pink, luscious yellow, sea blue, vivid orange, stunning lavender and pure white. These majestic plants make colorful borders and are also important elements in planning the background for permanent flower beds and landscapes.

Some shrubs have beautiful multicolored berries and others a range of foliage colors which add exciting seasonal color changes. Useful, too, are the fresh looking, all-green foliage plants which can add an atmosphere of clipped formality.

When selecting shrubs for any location it would be wise to learn about the plant's characteristics of growth and its needs: type of soil, amounts of sun and moisture, what are the expected habits of growth—fast, open or compact; slow upright or spreading; what size is expected at maturity?

Shrubs may be purchased either with bare roots or with the roots incased in a ball of earth wrapped in burlap. Balled and burlapped (often referred to as "B & B") are the most common. They may be moved and transplanted at any time (if given some protection from the hot sun), but do best if planted during the dormant season.

Before planting your shrub, be sure to dig a hole at least twice the size of the earth ball around the roots. Set the top soil aside to be placed later in the bottom of the hole. Mix the top soil with peat moss, well-rotted compost and a balanced fertilizer.

After the shrub is in place, cut the burlap from around the trunk and carefully fold it back . . . *do not* remove it. Fill and pack the surrounding hole until it is half full. Then, fill the hole with water. Wiggle the shrub and pat the earth around it to settle any

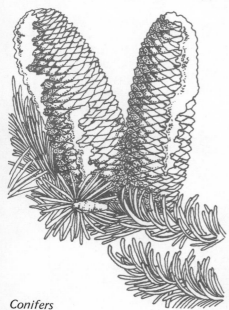

Conifers

air pockets. Continue to fill the hole leaving the surface in a saucer shape that can catch and hold water. Prune any broken or unshapely branches and paint every cut or wound with a tree dressing paint. Tender loving care the first two years after planting usually assures a well-started plant.

A cultivated area around the shrub prevents competition. But, do not dig too close to the roots which are usually shallow and can be easily damaged. Use a good mulch around the base of the shrub and keep weeds and grass pulled out by hand.

SHRUBS		
Flowering	Althea Azalea Beauty Bush Bluebeard Bridalwreath Broom Camelia Deutzia Dogwood Forsythia Gardenia Hibiscus Hydrangea	Lilac Magnolia Mock orange Oleander Peony Quince Rhododendron Snowball Spirea Star Magnolia Tamarisk Trumpet Vine Weigela
Berried	Barberry Climbing bittersweet Cranberry cotoneaster Evergreen blueberry Holly Holly grape Japonica Partridgeberry	Pernettya Pyracantha Red chokeberry Sea buckthorn Snowberry Spotted laurel Strawberry tree Viburnum
Evergreen	Alpine Currant Arborvitae Aucuba Boxwood Euonymus Hemlock Junipers	Lantana Ligustrum Mugho Pine Privet Spruce Yew Yucca

PIERIS (ANDROMEDA)

Specific Variety: *Japonica, Lily-of-the-Valley.*
Temperature Zone: *7.*
What To Plant: *Shrubs.*
When To Plant: *Spring or early fall.*
Type Of Soil: *Equal amounts of peat moss and soil or leaf mold and soil in well-drained acid bed.*
How To Plant: *Dig holes large enough to spread roots evenly.*
Watering Instructions: *As needed.*

Other Information: One of the wests most distinguished shrubs in form. Do not crowd.

Mrs. William Engelke, Pres.
Friendly Garden Club
Seattle, Washington

EUONYMUS

Specific Variety: *Variegated, yellow and green leaves.*
Temperature Zone: *8.*
What To Plant: *Shrub.*
When To Plant: *Spring.*
Type Of Soil: *Peat moss and humus mixed with good garden soil.*
How To Plant: *Plant in a large hole to*

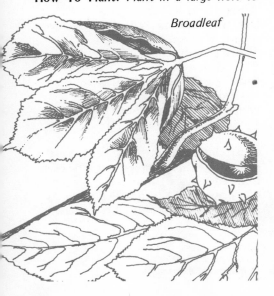

Broadleaf

allow roots to spread.
Watering Instructions: *Water generously before hole is completely filled to settle the soil. Water as needed thereafter.*
Fertilizing Instructions: *Good garden fertilizer such as 8-8-8.*
Pruning Instructions: *Prune or shape before new growth begins in spring.*

Other Information: Euonymus scale is very common, but may be controlled by spraying in late winter with Volck oil and in June with isotox. Scale may be recognized by symptoms of leaves turning yellow and dropping off. Shrubs appear to be covered by snow.

Mrs. John Q. Davis, Treas.
Canterbury Bells Garden Club
Montgomery, Alabama

BURNING BUSH (ALATUS)

Temperature Zone: *8.*
What To Plant: *Shrubs.*
When To Plant: *January through March.*
Type Of Soil: *Good loamy soil mixed with peat moss and compost.*
How To Plant: *Dig holes deeper and larger than roots of shrubs in sunny bed. Combine peat moss, compost and soil in bottom of holes, mixing well. Set shrubs out, spreading roots evenly, at original planting depth.*
Watering Instructions: *Water well when planted and whenever soil becomes dry.*
Fertilizing Instructions: *8-8-8 or any other good balanced fertilizer in spring when new growth begins, 0-14-14 in late fall.*
Pruning Instructions: *Prune just enough to shape.*

Other Information: Burning Bush is a beautiful, easily grown shrub that is evergreen in spring and summer with fiery red leaves and berries in fall.

Mrs. C. P. McClinton, Pres.
East Lake Garden Club
Birmingham, Alabama

MOUNTAIN LAUREL

Specific Variety: *Wild.*
Temperature Zone: *8.*
When To Plant: *January.*
Type Of Soil: *Soil enriched with leaf mold.*
How To Plant: *Transplant to previous growing depth.*
Watering Instructions: *Rain water if possible.*
Fertilizing Instructions: *Rotten wood and leaves.*
Pruning Instructions: *Prune to desired size after blooming.*

Mrs. A. R. Bethea, VP
Pioneer Garden Club
Flomaton, Alabama

RHODODENDRON CAROLINEANUM

Specific Variety: *P.J.M. hybrids.*
Temperature Zone: *3.*
What To Plant: *Plants.*
When To Plant: *Spring.*
Type Of Soil: *Acid.*
How To Plant: *Dig holes about twice the size of balled roots. Plant at nursery level.*
Watering Instructions: *As needed.*
Fertilizing Instructions: *None if soil has adequate humus.*
Pruning Instructions: *As desired to shape.*

Other Information: P.J.M. will grow to 3 or 4 feet. Plants have glossy green leaves in summer and mahogany-colored leaves in winter. Flowers are a bright lavender pink.

Velma Coyne
Ann Arbor Garden Club
Ann Arbor, Michigan

PHOTINIA

Specific Variety: *Serrulata.*
Temperature Zone: *9.*
What To Plant: *Shrubs.*

When To Plant: *Spring or early fall.*
Type Of Soil: *Sandy slightly acid loam.*
How To Plant: *Dig holes deep enough to spread roots in a sunny bed. Plant shrubs, pressing soil around shrubs firmly.*
Watering Instructions: *Water thoroughly when planting and whenever dry thereafter.*
Fertilizing Instructions: *Fertilize sparingly with fertilizer that contains trace elements.*
Pruning Instructions: *Prune severely when new growth develops for added leaf color.*

Other Information: Do not prune as severely if berries and flowers are desired on shrub. Spray with fungicide for mildew, if necessary.

Rachel Setchfield
Floretum Garden Club
Edmonds, Washington

POLYGONUM

Specific Variety: *Rosy red feather-like flowers in late summer.*
Temperature Zone: *8.*
What To Plant: *Shrubs.*
When To Plant: *Spring.*
Type Of Soil: *Well-drained light soil.*
How To Plant: *Shallow. Dig holes deep enough to spread roots.*
Watering Instructions: *Water only the first several days.*
Fertilizing Instructions: *Regular garden fertilizer such as 8-8-8.*
Pruning Instructions: *Prune only to shape or reduce size of bush.*

Other Information: Cut bush to the ground after first cold weather. The beautiful red flowers are pretty on the bush, but may be cut and dried for indoor arrangements. The dried flowers last indefinitely.

Mrs. Ouida Hicks
Star Jasmine Garden Club
Montgomery, Alabama

CORAL TREE

Specific Variety: *Erythrina Herbacea.*
Temperature Zone: *8.*
What To Plant: *Roots or seeds.*
When To Plant: *Fall or winter.*
Type Of Soil: *Sunny, well-drained soil.*
How To Plant: *Dig holes large enough for roots.*
Watering Instructions: *Water when planted.*
Fertilizing Instructions: *Not necessary to fertilize.*
Pruning Instructions: *Prune to keep within necessary space.*

Other Information: The Coral Tree has small sharp thorns and is sometimes called Devil-in-the-Bush or Flea-Weed. Bright crimson flowers bloom in spring and beautiful scarlet seeds grow in the fall.

Mrs. James McClure, Grounds Com.
Natchez Garden Club
Natchez, Mississippi

MAGNOLIAS

Specific Variety: *Star.*
Temperature Zone: *7.*
What To Plant: *Shrubs.*
When To Plant: *Spring.*
Type Of Soil: *Well-drained light soil.*
How To Plant: *Dig hole large enough for complete root spread.*
Watering Instructions: *Water well when planting.*
Fertilizing Instructions: *All-purpose fertilizer in early spring.*
Pruning Instructions: *Prune only to shape.*

Other Information: Star magnolia is a slow growing shrub that is fine for borders and entry-way gardens or edge of woods. Shrub is quite hardy but flowers are often nipped by frost.

Mrs. Donald Blake, Past Pres.
Hillsdale Garden Club
Tacoma, Washington

DWARF POINCIANA

Specific Variety: *Dwarf.*
Temperature Zone: *8.*
What To Plant: *Seeds.*
When To Plant: *Plant seeds in early spring or earlier in hot house to transplant later.*
Type Of Soil: *Clay or any type dry soil.*
How To Plant: *Plant seeds about 1/2 inch deep and reset when several inches tall.*
Watering Instructions: *Water as needed.*
Fertilizing Instructions: *Any fertilizer that can be used on most outdoor plants.*
Pruning Instructions: *Prune after sap goes down. Very little pruning is required.*

Other Information: The poinciana is the sacred flower of Siva in India. It has fiery red flowers that grow in clusters and blooms most of the year. Can be bought in tree variety or shrubs. There are many of these in Montgomery.

Mrs. M. H. Adourian, Federation Dir.
Star Jasmine Club
Montgomery, Alabama

LILAC (SYRINGA)

Specific Variety: *French hybrid lilac budded to privet ligustrum.*
Temperature Zone: *7.*
When To Plant: *Budding should be done between July and October.*
Type Of Soil: *Any good garden soil, more alkaline than acid.*
How To Plant: *Use same budding technique as used on roses.*
Watering Instructions: *Keep well-watered until budding is assured.*
Fertilizing Instructions: *Moderate fertilizing, leaning toward alkaline.*
Pruning Instructions: *Slight, wait until well established.*

Other Information: Budding a lilac on a privet root will do well with no special care but watering well.

Helen Morrill
Glad Hands Garden Club
Beaverton, Oregon

GRANNY GRAY BEARD

Specific Variety: *Wild.*
Temperature Zone: *8.*
What To Plant: *Seedlings or cuttings.*
When To Plant: *Spring.*
Type Of Soil: *Fertile moist soil in flickering shade or full sun.*
How To Plant: *Plant in spot as near as possible to the trees natural environment.*
Watering Instructions: *Water well until established.*
Fertilizing Instructions: *Once a year in late winter using any good fertilizer, rotted manure or leaf mold.*

Other Information: Find small seedlings around parent tree or make cuttings from pruning a limb below the bud. This shrub is a member of the olive family with black berries in the fall. Berries will sprout if soaked in water and planted in damp place. Shell should be carefully pierced for quicker results. Shrub is covered with a shawl of white spun moss in spring.

Mrs. Frank Eskridge, Pres.
Pioneer Garden Club
Flomaton, Alabama

HIBISCUS

Specific Variety: *Super giants.*
Temperature Zone: *7.*
What To Plant: *Shrubs.*
When To Plant: *Spring or fall.*
Type Of Soil: *Rich, well-drained soil.*
How To Plant: *Full sun, 3 feet apart.*
Watering Instructions: *Keep moist.*
Fertilizing Instructions: *Well-balanced fertilizer in spring.*
Pruning Instructions: *Prune back to ground in late fall.*

Other Information: Easily grown, spectacular results. Blooms are 10-12 inches in diameter.

Mrs. Walter H. Kaelin
Mesilla Valley Garden Club
Las Cruces, New Mexico

HYDRANGEA MACROPHYLLA

Specific Variety: *French type.*
Temperature Zone: *6.*
What To Plant: *Cuttings of half matured wood or root divisions.*
When To Plant: *Spring or autumn.*
Type Of Soil: *Rich, moist soil.*
How To Plant: *Deep dig holes large enough to spread roots.*
Watering Instructions: *Water at planting time and weekly thereafter during dry weather.*
Fertilizing Instructions: *Cow manure or 5-10-5.*
Pruning Instructions: *Prune after flowering, removing all weak growth and dead wood.*

Other Information: The addition of peat moss, leaf mold and sand aids in producing blue flowers. Water with a solution of 3 ounces of aluminum sulphate to 1 gallon of water. Tie up branches and bank soil around bases for winter protection. Cover tops with hardwood leaves, oak or ash. Mature flowers dry beautifully for arrangements.

Mrs. Harold G. Phillips
Pub. Rel. Chm., Past Pres.
Garden Club of Wyoming Valley
Kingston, Pennsylvania

PEONIES

Specific Variety: *Singles or doubles.*
Temperature Zone: *7.*
What To Plant: *Strong healthy roots.*
When To Plant: *Fall.*
Type Of Soil: *Good garden loam in well-drained beds.*
How To Plant: *Mulch soil well. Taper holes so the roots will not sink. Plant crowns not more than 1 inch below surface.*
Watering Instructions: *Water as needed.*
Fertilizing Instructions: *Feed generously with organic or barnyard fertilizer.*
Pruning Instructions: *Prune tops and burn plants after they have died down.*

Other Information: Peonies do not like to be moved. Blooming period may be extended by buying early, midseason and late varieties. Large flowering varieties may need supports.

Mrs. Edwin Richards, Pres.
Estacada Garden Club
Oregon City, Oregon

PEONIES

Temperature Zone: *6.*
What To Plant: *Roots with at least 3 eyes.*
When To Plant: *September through October.*
Type Of Soil: *Good heavy garden loam.*
How To Plant: *Dig holes to depth of 2 feet. Fill lower part with topsoil mixed with humus, manure, compost and peat moss. Set roots out with eyes not more than 2 inches below soil.*
Watering Instructions: *Water if season is dry.*
Fertilizing Instructions: *Fork rotted manure lightly into ground around plants in the spring. Add 5-10-5 fertilizer and wood ash.*
Pruning Instructions: *Cut flowers when faded. Cut down to ground level in fall; do away with foliage, trying not to leave a stubble.*

Other Information: Peonies have been known to bloom more than 50 years in 1 spot. Do not move often. Peonies like an open sunny location although they will do alright with some shade. Ground should be well drained. Spray with Bordeaux mixture 2 or 3 times at 10-day intervals in the spring.

Mrs. Leonard H. Tebbe
Mt Healthy Garden Club
Cincinnati, Ohio

PEONIES

Specific Variety: *Mons Jules Elie, Festiva Maxima, Mrs. Bryce Fontaine.*

Peony

Temperature Zone: *5.*
What To Plant: *Root divisions.*
When To Plant: *Fall.*
Type Of Soil: *Light well-drained garden soil.*
How To Plant: *Dig large holes. Mix soil with plenty of bone meal. Place root with eyes 2 inches below top of soil. Water well.*
Watering Instructions: *Do not sprinkle during blooming period; irrigate with ditches at that time.*
Fertilizing Instructions: *Plenty of bone meal and hardwood ashes. Barnyard fertilizer may be used once every few years.*
Pruning Instructions: *Foliage should be cut close to ground in the fall.*

Other Information: Peonies need plenty of sun. It is important to spray when plants first start to grow in the spring. Use a sprinkling can with a Bordeaux mixture. Repeat in 10 days or two weeks. Single varieties are fabulous in arrangements.

Mrs. Merlin Fitch
East Wenatchee Garden Club
Wenatchee, Washington

PEONIES

Specific Variety: *Kansas, Early Spring, Double Red.*
Temperature Zone: *8.*
What To Plant: *Root divisions.*
When To Plant: *Late September or October.*
Type Of Soil: *Well-drained garden loam.*
How To Plant: *Shallow with eyes at ground level; barely cover. Dig holes at least 1 1/2 feet deep and same width. Spread roots over mounds in bottom of holes; water and cover.*
Watering Instructions: *Water well when planted and whenever dry.*
Fertilizing Instructions: *Mix peat moss, compost and bone meal in bottom of hole when planting. Light application of bone meal in spring, handful over each plant after tops are cut off to leave over winter.*
Pruning Instructions: *Cut to ground when tops have dried.*

Other Information: Do not let seed buds develop and mature as this takes strength from the plant. Spray very early in spring with Bordeaux mixture to keep down Botrytis. If plants are doing well do not move. Can go many years without dividing if about 3 feet is allowed between plants.

Mrs. C. P. McClinton, Pres.
East Lake Garden Club
Birmingham, Alabama

PEONIES

Specific Variety: *Red Emperor, Nippon Gold, Mary May, Early Red, Martha Bullock.*
Temperature Zone: *4.*
What To Plant: *Divisions with 3 eyes.*
When To Plant: *Late August or September.*
Type Of Soil: *Ordinary soil, good drainage essential.*
How To Plant: *Dig holes 12 to 18 inches deep; put several handfuls of bone meal in bottom of holes. Cover with rich soil. Plant peony eyes 2 inches deep.*
Watering Instructions: *Water well at time of planting.*
Fertilizing Instructions: *A little bone meal may be added around plants and worked lightly into the soil each spring.*
Pruning Instructions: *Leaves are left on plants until late fall; cut off after first frost.*

Other Information: Peonies prefer full sun but may take light shade. Mulch the 1st winter after planting in very cold climates. Peonies must not have eyes more than 2 inches deep or they will not blossom.

Mrs. A. D. Kellogg
Homer Garden Club
Homer, Michigan

SHADBUSH
(AMELANCHIER)

Temperature Zone: *5.*
What To Plant: *Shrubs.*
When To Plant: *Spring.*
Type Of Soil: *Moist or damp soil.*
How To Plant: *Dig holes to spread roots.*
Watering Instructions: *Plant in damp spot.*

Other Information: This bush is a good one for a damp, soggy spot. They are also good along streams or woodlands. Plant has white flowers in late spring, then bears fruit the birds love. The foliage is yellow in autumn.

Peggy West, W and M Chm.
Sharon Hill Garden Club
Coraopolis, Pennsylvania

SALIX DISCOLOR

Specific Variety: *Pussy Willow.*
Temperature Zone: *4.*
What To Plant: *Rooted branch.*
When To Plant: *Spring.*
Type Of Soil: *Moist sandy to loamy soils.*
How To Plant: *Place branch in water*

until roots show; plant in desired spot.
Watering Instructions: *Keep wet until leaves are fully out and growing.*
Fertilizing Instructions: *Any good shrub fertilizer or rich compost and Driconure.*
Pruning Instructions: *Shape as desired.*

Other Information: Cut back every 4 or 5 years almost to trunk section. The new growth is healthier and has larger catkins. Spray with Ortho and isotox each March; continue monthly until leaves fall.

Mary Sue Wion, Horticulturist
Livonia Garden Club
Livonia, Michigan

SCARLET FLOWERING QUINCE

Temperature Zone: *6.*
What To Plant: *Shrubs.*
When To Plant: *Fall or spring.*
Type Of Soil: *Any good soil.*
How To Plant: *Dig holes large enough for shrubs. Place peat moss and Rap-id-Gro in holes, mixing well with soil. Mound soil in bottom of holes; place shrubs on mounds, spreading roots evenly. Water well; fill with soil.*
Watering Instructions: *Every 3 or 4 days if dry.*
Fertilizing Instructions: *Rap-id-Gro.*
Pruning Instructions: *Cut branches when blooming to use in arrangements or to shape the bush.*

Other Information: Very hardy bush, not bothered by insects.

Mrs. Howard Pomeroy
Mammoth Spring Garden Club
Mammoth Spring, Arkansas

PRIMROSE

Specific Variety: *Polyanthus.*
Temperature Zone: *8.*
What To Plant: *Seeds or plant divisions.*
When To Plant: *Late March or early April.*
Type Of Soil: *Good garden soil.*

How To Plant: *Start seeds under apple tree, cover with sand and burlap bag. Primroses grow well with rhododendrons.*
Watering Instructions: *Never let seed bed dry out.*
Fertilizing Instructions: *Rotted cow manure, compost and leaf mold.*
Pruning Instructions: *Divide after blooming. If plants get too big the blooms will be small.*

Other Information: When planting seeds, moisten seeds and freeze, then let thaw. Repeat several times before planting. Plants do well on north side of house or in partial shade. Primroses go dormant in summer; will bloom again in fall. Diazanon is good bait for slugs and strawberry weevils.

Mrs. Oscar Sundberg, Past Pres.
Greenwood Garden Club
Stanwood, Washington

WEIGELA

Specific Variety: *Esperance.*
Temperature Zone: *8.*
What To Plant: *Shrubs.*
When To Plant: *December through February.*
Type Of Soil: *Any good garden soil.*
How To Plant: *Dig holes large enough for roots to spread out. Combine sand and peat moss; place in bottom of holes.*
Watering Instructions: *Fill holes with water when planting to soak into soil.*
Fertilizing Instructions: *Work 8-8-8 into soil around but not on roots in fall and again in January. Apply again after blooming season.*
Pruning Instructions: *Trim out old wood after flowering.*

Other Information: This shrub has beautiful clusters of bell-shaped flowers that spread. Be sure shrub has plenty of room to grow.

Mrs. Robert E. Kelly, Bd. of Trustees
Montgomery Federation of Garden Clubs, Inc.
Montgomery, Alabama

AZALEAS

Specific Variety: *Indica.*
Temperature Zone: *6.*
What To Plant: *Shrubs.*
When To Plant: *Late winter, spring.*
Type Of Soil: *Well-drained acid soil containing humus.*
How To Plant: *Dig shallow holes much larger than plants to spread roots.*
Watering Instructions: *Requires constant moisture with good drainage.*
Fertilizing Instructions: *Cottonseed meal plus a heavy mulch of pine needles and oak leaves.*
Pruning Instructions: *Prune to keep at desired size and to produce more flowers.*

Other Information: Azaleas are almost bug proof and do best in filtered sunlight. They are long lasting as a cut flower and suited for small gardens or large estates. Use as an accent plant around pools, in hedges or as a foundation plant.

Mrs. Frank Weight, 1st VP
Plain Dirt Gardeners
Newport, Arkansas

AZALEAS

Specific Variety: *Dwarf.*
Temperature Zone: *7.*
What To Plant: *Shrubs.*
When To Plant: *Anytime from December to February.*
Type Of Soil: *Well-drained light soil.*
How To Plant: *Dig shallow holes large enough to spread roots. Shape mounds in holes. Place plants on mounds, spreading roots. Cover plants with soil.*
Watering Instructions: *Water year-round if soil becomes dry.*
Fertilizing Instructions: *Fertilize with azalea and camellia fertilizer after blooming and again in the fall. Add 1 tablespoon sulphur and 1 tablespoon iron sulphate twice a year.*
Pruning Instructions: *Prune, if necessary, after blooming.*

Other Information: Be careful not to hoe around shrubs at any time as roots are on top of ground and do not like to be disturbed. Spray with Malathon and oil emulsion in the spring and fall before temperature reaches 65 degrees.

Mrs. Odell Clary, Pres.
Rose Garden Club
Bradley, Arkansas

AZALEAS

Specific Variety: *Exbury hybrids.*
Temperature Zone: *8.*
What To Plant: *Seeds.*
When To Plant: *Anytime.*
How To Plant: *Plant seeds in plastic trays or pots in sterilized compost and peat moss. Cover with sand. Transplant seedlings to larger flats when plants have 6 leaves. Move to permanent place of growth when 6 inches high. Bloom can be expected in 3 years.*
Watering Instructions: *Keep soil moist; cover with Kleenex until seedlings are up.*
Fertilizing Instructions: *Do not fertilize until ready to transplant. Use acid fertilizer.*
Pruning Instructions: *Do not prune except to remove old dead wood. Never cultivate under plants.*

Mrs. Kenneth Harbow, Pres.
Juliana Garden Club
Cottage Grove, Oregon

AZALEAS

Specific Variety: *Indica, Pride of Mobile, Formosa.*
Temperature Zone: *8.*
What To Plant: *Shrubs.*
When To Plant: *Preferably at bloom time in spring or in fall.*
Type Of Soil: *Acid soil, pH 4.5 to 6.5, holes filled with loose and friable humus. Add leaf mold and peat moss.*
How To Plant: *Shallow planting with roots spread near the surface of soil is best; water and mulch.*
Watering Instructions: *Water well in dry*

season, when buds are forming and before a cold spell.

Fertilizing Instructions: *Feed liberally after blooming with camellia and azalea fertilizer. Do not cultivate as roots are near the surface.*

Pruning Instructions: *Prune after blooming season to keep in bounds.*

Other Information: Azaleas do well in sun or partial shade. Lace bugs or spider mites may be controlled by oil base sprays. Azalea gall is characterized by thickened, fleshy growths in the leaves, flowers and twigs, usually in spring. Galls should be cut out and plants sprayed with a good fungicide.

Mrs. W. R. McNeill
Camellia Garden Club
Montgomery, Alabama

CAMELLIAS

Specific Variety: *Empress.*
Temperature Zone: *8.*

Camellia

What To Plant: *Shrubs.*
When To Plant: *Fall.*
Type Of Soil: *Light loam.*
How To Plant: *2 feet wide deep holes.*
Watering Instructions: *Water frequently in late summer and early fall.*
Fertilizing Instructions: *8-8-8.*
Pruning Instructions: *In fall as needed.*

Mrs. W. A. Salter
East Lake Garden Club
Birmingham, Alabama

CAMELLIA JAPONICA

Specific Variety: *Evergreen shrub with single to semi-double blooms.*
Temperature Zone: *8.*
What To Plant: *Shrubs.*
When To Plant: *Fall.*
Type Of Soil: *Light, acid soil abundantly supplied with organic matter.*
How To Plant: *Plant in raised beds. Dig holes large enough to spread roots. Do not plant too deep.*
Watering Instructions: *Soil should be kept moist at all times but never allowed to become soggy.*
Fertilizing Instructions: *2 to 3 feedings are recommended after the blooming period is over. Five parts cottonseed meal, 3 parts superphosphate and 2 parts sulphate of potash are recommended.*
Pruning Instructions: *Prune only to remove dead wood and to improve the shapeliness of bush.*

Other Information: Camellias should be mulched in order to conserve the moisture in the soil and to afford protection for the roots which tend to be near the surface. Use peat moss, oak leaf mold, pine needles and acid compost. Spray with oil emulsion in early spring for scales. After April use Cygon. Protect camellias from cold if planted along the northern limit of the camellia belt.

Mrs. F. M. Thornton, Pres.
Spade and Hope Garden Club
Elton, Louisiana

CAMELLIA JAPONICA

Specific Variety: *Pink Perfection.*
Temperature Zone: *7.*
When To Plant: *March to late June.*
Type Of Soil: *Sandy loam enriched with compost and sphagnum peat moss.*
How To Plant: *Prepare planting holes ahead with equal parts sand, loam, peat moss and compost. Let soil settle. Plant with root ball 1 or 2 inches above ground level. Fill in and around with soil mixture. Mulch deeply with pine needles or ground bark.*
Watering Instructions: *Water foliage and ground well when dry.*
Fertilizing Instructions: *Hollytone early in spring. Never fertilize after June 1st.*
Pruning Instructions: *Cut blooms in spring. Remove all except 1 or 2 buds from each branch in fall.*

Other Information: Camellias should be planted to protect naturally from winter sun and wind. Camellias will sulk if planted 1 inch too deep and die if 2 inches too deep. Camellias cannot stand drought nor to stand in water. Maintain mulch year round. A joy to behold when in bloom.

Mrs. John W. Burris, Life Judge, EIP Chm.
Sussex Gardeners
Rehobth Beach, Delaware

FRINGE BUSH
(CHIONANTHUS)

Specific Variety: *Chinese.*
What To Plant: *Shrubs, seeds or cuttings.*
When To Plant: *Early spring in a sunny place.*
Type Of Soil: *Deep loamy soil enriched with decayed manure.*
Watering Instructions: *Water well until shrub gets started.*
Fertilizing Instructions: *Decayed organic matter.*
Pruning Instructions: *Prune around unless tall plants are desired. Prune at bottom for tall plants.*

Other Information: White flowers are freely borne in loose panicles 5 to 9 inches long.

Mrs. Ruth Woolum, Treas.
Sun Valley Garden Club
Kitts Hill, Ohio

JUNIPERS

Specific Variety: *Creeping junipers.*
Temperature Zone: *4.*
What To Plant: *Cuttings or shrubs.*
When To Plant: *Early spring.*
Type Of Soil: *Fertile loam pH 6.5-7.0.*
How To Plant: *Cut 8-inch healthy branches from shrub; strip all needles from lower 4 or 5 inches of the branches. Plant in sand or rich dirt in shade with only top 3 to 4 inches out of ground. Plant shrubs in good loam in 6-inch pots. Plant pots in shade. May transplant in 2 years.*
Watering Instructions: *Keep soil moist but never waterlogged.*

Elton Lux, Proj. Chm.
Garden Club of Lincoln
Lincoln, Nebraska

YEW (TAXUS)

What To Plant: *Shrubs.*
When To Plant: *Spring or fall.*
Type Of Soil: *Well-drained soil.*
How To Plant: *Dig large holes; plant root balls.*
Watering Instructions: *Water around roots. Do not allow to dry out until established.*
Fertilizing Instructions: *5-10-5.*
Pruning Instructions: *Prune to shape after a year.*

Other Information: Yews come in upright or spreading shapes and are easy to grow. Place 1 or 2 empty orange shells in center of plants to keep dogs off. Will work for other shrubs too.

Mrs. Kenneth R. Garvick, Credentials Chm.
Heritage Garden Club
Natl. Council of State Garden Clubs
Mansfield, Ohio

SPREADING YEW
(TAXUS CUSPIDATA)

Specific Variety: *Taxus Cuspidata.*
Temperature Zone: *3.*
What To Plant: *Seedlings or 3-year old plants.*
When To Plant: *Early spring.*
Type Of Soil: *Good black loam.*
How To Plant: *Dig holes large enough to spread roots. Mix compost with soil for filling holes.*
Watering Instructions: *Water well when first planted and once a week the first year.*
Fertilizing Instructions: *Place compost on top of soil; mix in lightly.*
Pruning Instructions: *Prune only to shape or thicken the first 5 years. May use branches for arrangements.*

Other Information: Trees have red berries which are poisonous to humans.

Mrs. W. E. Meyer
Bancroft Garden Club
Bancroft, Nebraska

PYRACANTHA

Specific Variety: *Lalandi.*
Temperature Zone: *4.*
What To Plant: *Shrubs.*
When To Plant: *Spring.*
Type Of Soil: *Well-drained soil.*
How To Plant: *Dig holes large enough to spread roots.*
Watering Instructions: *Water several times until established and after that only as needed.*
Fertilizing Instructions: *1 cup of super-phosphate and 1 cup 5-10-5 each spring.*
Pruning Instructions: *Cut the largest stem as close to the ground as possible each spring after the shrubs are well established. Shrubs may be espaliered, if desired.*

Mrs. G. L. Litzenberg, Past Pres.
The Garden Club of Lincoln
Lincoln, Nebraska

Pyracantha

PYRACANTHA

Specific Variety: *Scarlet Firethorn.*
Temperature Zone: *5.*
What To Plant: *Shrubs.*
When To Plant: *Early spring or autumn.*
Type Of Soil: *Well-drained soil. Plants like lime and plenty of leaf mold.*
How To Plant: *Dig holes large enough to accommodate spreading root system. Plant at medium depth in open sun.*
Watering Instructions: *Water well after planting and frequently thereafter until plants have become established.*
Fertilizing Instructions: *Well-rotted barnyard manure and leaf mulch.*
Pruning Instructions: *Prune in early spring or during the last weeks of winter, removing surplus stems at base of plant.*

Other Information: Pyracantha hedges keep down traffic noises, provide privacy, afford food and shelter for numerous birds and is a year-round delight. Berries last well into winter.

Mrs. Fred Mauntel
Washington Garden Club
Natl. Coun. of State Garden Clubs, Past Pres.
Washington, Missouri

Special Gardens

Although most people think of a garden as a lovely outdoor landscape of green foliage and brightly colored blossoms, anyone can create a perfect garden in miniature . . . a beautiful hanging basket for a city window, a flourishing rock garden for a steep terrace, a fragrant herb garden for the apartment kitchen, or a spectacular terrarium for any room in the house.

Everyone loves the beauty and freshness of the outdoors—and what better way to have this artistry of nature in your home than with living plants. Special gardens for indoor use are really not very expensive and their living green elegance can add so much to a family room.

You can use hanging baskets in almost any room in the house or on patio and porch areas. These baskets can be bought at local retail stores in many colors, sizes, shapes and materials. You might want to make your own, using shallow flower pots hung by the latest macrame' knots. Actually, since most hanging basket plants will eventually cover the container, almost any holder that allows for proper drainage will make a good hanging basket.

There are so many beautiful plants from which to choose . . . any size and shape imaginable . . . solid green or variegated . . . flowers in every color of the rainbow. You can select from many varieties of ferns, cascading ivy, colorful Red Raspberry, Begonias in all shades, pale green fig vines, an unusual-shaped spider plant, and a very simple Philodendron.

Of course, miniature gardens or landscapes will also be an addition to your home and can really become an interesting conversation piece. These can be planted in shallow bowls or trays and can portray almost any type landscape.

Cacti, very popular in miniature garden scenery, come in varieties of shapes and sizes, some spindled with thorns and pricks and others with attractive, colorful blooms.

In making miniature gardens, originality is one of the real keys to success. Style and symmetry are the most important factors. Make use of nursery plants or collect your own wild mosses and grasses. Arrange your plants around an eyecatcher—a piece

Hanging Garden

of driftwood, a dark rock, a small figurine or building. For a varied landscape, build up hills and carve out valleys. Most important—do not overdo.

Another special garden that can really be fun for the whole family is the rock garden or "rockery." These many-leveled, artistically planted gardens of alpine flowers (for cool climates), and dwarf or miniature plants elsewhere, can range from massive gardens covering an entire hillside to a small man-made section of a door-yard garden of a collection of small pots.

In choosing a site for your rock garden, it is wise to use an already sloping area. Most alpine flowers cannot tolerate poor drainage or dripping water from overhanging tree branches. They also will not thrive if exposed to dry gusty winds.

There is one important rule to remember in selecting the type of stone for your rock garden . . . Use local stone if it is durable and attractive. This stone—which of course will be much cheaper than imported rocks will usually look more natural. Lava rocks which are light in weight are now available from most nurseries.

After the garden is complete, the beginner should select plants that are both easy to grow and lovely to look at. Leave the more difficult varieties of alpine flowers until your increasing skills enable you to deal with their temperamental behavior.

Terrariums, once the province of Victorian parlors, are currently enjoying a resurgence of popularity. These miniature gardens under glass provide delightful green vistas throughout the bleakest months of winter. Inexpensive and easily maintained, terrariums are fun to plant and provide a continuing source of pleasure for all ages.

A terrarium is technically a miniature greenhouse in which the humidity and temperature can be easily controlled, making it possible for a wide variety of small plants to thrive. Because terrariums are becoming fashionable there is no problem finding a wide selection of containers and plants for sale at many local retail stores.

The only basic requirement of a terrarium container is that it be made of clear glass or plastic. These materials will allow the passage of sufficient light for healthy plant growth. Often, one is tempted to make terrariums out of lovely old bottles made of tinted glass. However, unless the color is very muted, the light intensity is reduced and the colored glass tends to transmit its own hue while absorbing the other colors in the spectrum. This can cause abnormal growth or stunting in plants and failure of the terrarium.

Nearly any clear glass or plastic container will make a suitable terrarium. Various sizes of round, octagonal and rectangular fish aquariums . . . bottles of all sizes and shapes . . . jars, vases, decanters, mugs, goblets, and pitchers are available. The size of the terrarium container is optional so long as the size of the plants are in keeping with the scale of the container.

Although the very term terrarium signifies a closed environment, opinions differ on the virtues of sealing the terrarium. If sealed, the moisture and humidity remain constant and the plants are protected against dust, molds and household fungi. An open terrarium is suitable for many plants but must be more carefully watched to prevent excessive drying. Any number of materials can be used to cover the opening . . . a sheet of glass, or a temporary plastic wrap makes unobtrusive seals. Decorative objects such as corks or glass stoppers can be used.

The proper choice of plants depends upon three main factors . . . the size and shape of the container . . . whether it is to be sealed or left open . . . and, the amount of light available to the plants. A good basic rule to follow is to select plants that require similar growing conditions. Plants should be chosen carefully for variety in height, color, texture and form. Slow growing dwarf plants insure long-time beauty.

You will want to use some tall and medium-sized plants as well as some tiny, low ground plants. Foliage may be big or small, broad or narrow, smooth or hairy. Colors may vary from deep green to yellow-green to variegated white. Accent plants of purple and shades of red add interest.

A note of caution: *Always* use distilled water in your terrarium.

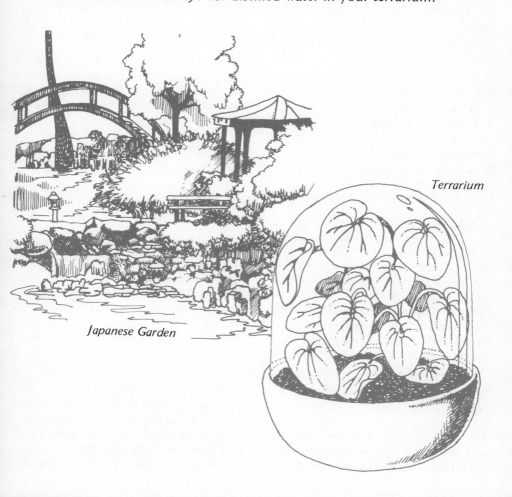

Terrarium

Japanese Garden

FUCHSIA

Specific Variety: *Trailing.*
What To Plant: *Rooted cuttings.*
When To Plant: *Spring.*
Type Of Soil: *Leaf mold mixed with potting soil.*
How To Plant: *Set out 3 to 4 plants in basket; hang in shade.*
Watering Instructions: *Soak daily. Spray foliage 2 or 3 times a day in hot weather.*
Fertilizing Instructions: *0-10-10 once weekly.*
Pruning Instructions: *Pinch tips to thicken plants.*

Other Information: May be left out until first light frost, then cut back to edge of basket and stored in frost free room. Keep damp all winter. Bring into light in March.

Betty Archer
Mountlake Terrace Garden Club
Alderwood Manor, Washington

FUCHSIA

Temperature Zone: *8.*
What To Plant: *Rooted cuttings.*
When To Plant: *Early spring.*
Type Of Soil: *Loose rich slightly acid soil.*
How To Plant: *Plant at original soil level in any type of hanging basket or planter for hanging.*
Watering Instructions: *Keep well watered with good drainage. Do not water new plantings too much.*
Fertilizing Instructions: *Half strength water soluable fertilizer every week.*
Pruning Instructions: *Prune after danger of frost is past; cut back to 2 or 3 nodes. Repot if necessary.*

Other Information: Pinch out the tip after growth starts and after the 3rd set of leaves have grown. Continue pruning until there is a nice full head and blossoms appear on new growth at the tips. Store in a frost free place for winter.

Water lightly. Fuchsias need to be grown in a sheltered place. They do not like full sun or drafts.

Mrs. Harry Epperson, Past Pres.
Hauser Garden Club
North Bend, Oregon

FUCHSIA

Specific Variety: *Trailing.*
Temperature Zone: *7.*
What To Plant: *Rooted cuttings.*
When To Plant: *Early spring.*
Type Of Soil: *Potting mixture.*
How To Plant: *Plant in hanging baskets; keep indoors until danger of frost is past.*
Watering Instructions: *Keep moist.*
Fertilizing Instructions: *Feed once a week with any good plant food.*

Other Information: All fuchsias kept through winter must be cut back to about 3 inches and left in a dry cool dark spot. Cuttings are an excellent way to start new plants for the next summer.

Mrs. Larry Schaut, Past Pres.
North Hill Garden Club
Seattle, Washington

HANGING BASKET TOMATOES

Specific Variety: *Cherry, Tiny Tim, Atom, Patio.*
Temperature Zone: *8.*
What To Plant: *Well-established plants.*
When To Plant: *Spring when danger of frost is past.*
Type Of Soil: *1/3 peat, 1/3 sand, 1/3 loam.*
How To Plant: *2 or 3 plants to a 10-inch pot. Place plants on slant to allow them to cascade.*
Watering Instructions: *Water 2 or 3 times a week in hot weather by placing basket in tub of water until container stops bubbling. Drip on grass and rehang.*
Fertilizing Instructions: *Feed with special*

tomato fertilizer according to directions on package.

Pruning Instructions: *Keep ripe fruit picked and basket will last until late fall.*

Other Information: Line hanging basket with damp spagnum moss and 4 layers of black nylon net cut in circles. Place mixed soil on net and plant tomatoes in basket. Place the stems under as much soil as possible enabling plants to form greater root system. Dwarf, Tiny Tim and Atom varieties tend to give upright growth. Cherry tomatoes grow horizontally and will cascade over the rim in a more graceful manner.

Mrs. James Durden, Pres.
Forsythia Garden Club
Montgomery, Alabama

SWEDISH IVY (PLECTRANTHUS)

What To Plant: *Vine.*
When To Plant: *Spring.*
Type Of Soil: *Plant in a mixture of soil, humus, peat moss and sand.*
How To Plant: *Make hole large enough to spread roots; cover with soil.*
Watering Instructions: *Keep evenly moist.*
Fertilizing Instructions: *Liquid fertilizer such as 7-14-7 following instructions on label.*
Pruning Instructions: *Prune to shape or reduce size of vine.*

Other Information: This vine is beautiful in a hanging basket. Cut runners into 4-inch pieces and root in water to start new plants.

Ruth Tyer, Horticulture Chm.
Twilight Garden Club
Washington, North Carolina

STRAWBERRY GERANIUM

Specific Variety: *Saxifraga Chinensis*
Temperature Zone: 7.
What To Plant: *Plants.*

Type Of Soil: *Potting soil or rich garden soil.*
How To Plant: *Plant in a hanging basket.*
Watering Instructions: *Let soil dry slightly between waterings.*
Fertilizing Instructions: *Fertilize only 3 times a year to keep good leaf color.*

Other Information: Plants have reddish runners which produce little plantlets in the air. Pin down to soil to start rooting. May also cut off and root in water and then pot. Light shade and relatively cool days and nights. Plant has a feminine delicacy not common to most cascading hanging plants.

Mrs. Jerald T. Lewis, Past Treas.
Hillsdale Garden Club
Tacoma, Washington

EVERBEARING STRAWBERRIES

Specific Variety: *Ozark Beauty, Osallala.*
Temperature Zone: 6.
What To Plant: *Plants.*
When To Plant: *Spring.*
Type Of Soil: *Any well-drained soil.*
How To Plant: *Plant 18 inches apart in rows 3 feet apart. Space runners 6 to 7 inches apart, making an 18-inch wide row.*
Watering Instructions: *The first few days after planting.*
Fertilizing Instructions: *Requires very little fertilizer. Four pounds 5-10-5 to a 100-foot row.*
Pruning Instructions: *Pick off blossoms during first season of bed until July so plants will produce the desired number of runners.*

Other Information: Mulch the bed with 1 inch sawdust after the first cultivation and fertilizing. Weeds should be pulled out, not cut off or hoed.

Mrs. Joseph W. Shertzer, VP
The Lookout Garden Club
Rainelle, West Virginia

HERBS

Temperature Zone: *5.*
What To Plant: *Seeds, root cuttings, plant divisions.*
When To Plant: *Spring.*
Type Of Soil: *Good garden soil mixed with compost and rotted manure.*
How To Plant: *Start plants in pots in the house or greenhouse in winter or early spring; move to garden when weather permits.*
Watering Instructions: *Water when needed.*
Fertilizing Instructions: *No additional fertilizer needed if manure is used, otherwise 1 application of 10-6-4 or 8-8-8 fertilizer in spring.*
Pruning Instructions: *Pruning is achieved when cutting herbs for use. Remove in fall.*

Other Information: May use a series of 12-inch drain pipes approximately 24 inches long inserted into garden about 18 to 20 inches apart with large end about 4 to 6 inches above soil level. Put soil mixture into pipe to about same level as outside soil level and plant. Area between pipes may be cleaned of vegetation, covered with gravel or some other mulch and treated for weed control.

Kenneth E. Rentschler, Horticulturist
Cinti Hills Garden Club
Cincinnati, Ohio

HERBS

Specific Variety: *Kitchen variety.*
Temperature Zone: *8.*
What To Plant: *Seeds.*
When To Plant: *Spring when all danger of frost is past.*
Type Of Soil: *Loamy sweet soil with good drainage.*
How To Plant: *Plant in shallow drills; tamp soil over seeds. Keep moist during germination.*
Watering Instructions: *Water when earth*

Herb Garden

seems dry or plants wither.
Fertilizing Instructions: *Small amount of fertilizer if soil is poor. Too much fertilizer makes plants too vigorous.*
Pruning Instructions: *Cut blooms off as they appear. Never let plants go to seed.*

Other Information: Your gardening experience will be greatly enhanced by adding a few plants of the most used herbs to your garden. Rosemary, sage, parsley, chives, oregano, sweet marjoram and several mints are nice to grow.

Mrs. Richard A. Green, VP
Cherokee Rose Garden Club
Montgomery, Alabama

WILD FLOWER GARDEN

Specific Variety: *Indigenous herbs, shrubs, ferns.*
Temperature Zone: *8.*
When To Plant: *Early spring.*
Type Of Soil: *Friable, high leaf mold content.*
How To Plant: *Duplicate natural habitat as nearly as possible.*

Watering Instructions: *Water often enough to keep soil slightly moist.*
Fertilizing Instructions: *Leaf mold makes desirable mulch. Commercial fertilizer may kill plants.*

Other Information: A wild flower garden is interesting the year around. Bare branches are lovely during dormant period. Carefully chosen plants make your garden enjoyable every season.

Mrs. Thomas M. Miller, Pres.
Daffodil Garden Club
Dothan, Alabama

HERB GARDEN
IN RAISED BOX

Specific Variety: *Parsley, dill, sage, chives, sweet marjoram.*
Temperature Zone: *8.*
What To Plant: *Seeds or starter plants.*
When To Plant: *Early spring after frost.*
Type Of Soil: *Light sandy or garden loam.*
How To Plant: *Measure off desired space in sunny location and mark with string. Drive 4 wooden stakes treated with a preservative into ground at corners. Nail 1-inch thick stained and treated planks to stakes. Bottom boards should sink slightly into ground before soil is pushed back against them. Fill box with sandy soil or garden loam and plant seeds or plants. Plant seeds about 18 inches apart and 1/4 inch deep. Thin to 1 foot apart when plants are 3 inches tall.*
Watering Instructions: *Water when planting and when soil is dry to touch.*
Fertilizing Instructions: *Liquid ortho or 8-8-8.*
Pruning Instructions: *Pick herbs when they begin to ripen and store in a dry airy place.*

Mrs. J. Gaston Grimes, Past Pres.
Home and Garden Club
Lexington, North Carolina

MINIATURE GARDEN

Temperature Zone: *8.*
What To Plant: *Wild ferns, grasses, mosses, small plants.*
When To Plant: *Anytime.*
Type Of Soil: *Standard potting soil.*
How To Plant: *Plant in shallow bowl; fill with soil. Set out plants, arranging in pretty and natural fashion.*
Watering Instructions: *Water as needed when soil begins to dry.*
Fertilizing Instructions: *Plant food, following instructions on label.*

Other Information: Form miniature garden around an attractive rock or piece of driftwood. Place finished product in a partly sunny location where it can be enjoyed by all. Can be a fun project to gather as a family or group.

Barbara Tubbs, Pres.
Bonita Garden Club
Jones, Louisiana

MINIATURE LANDSCAPES

Temperature Zone: *8.*
What To Plant: *Young seedling trees, moss, grass.*
When To Plant: *Anytime.*
Type Of Soil: *Standard potting soil with charcoal layer on bottom for drainage.*
How To Plant: *Arrange charcoal and soil in tray; add a bridge if desired. Arrange plants around bridge.*
Watering Instructions: *Water as needed when soil begins to dry.*
Fertilizing Instructions: *Plant food.*

Other Information: Sprinkle plant material with sand or colored gravel. May use small figurines, animals or houses for an interesting landscape. Build up hills; carve out valleys for streams or hollows for ponds or lakes. Let your or your children's imaginations reign.

Barbara Tubbs, Pres.
Bonita Garden Club
Jones, Louisiana

EVERBEARING RED RASPBERRY

Specific Variety: *Crimson Thumb, Red Plumpies.*
Temperature Zone: *6.*
What To Plant: *Plants.*
When To Plant: *Early spring.*
Type Of Soil: *Fine sandy loam.*
How To Plant: *Set plants out 1 foot apart in 8 or 9-inch holes that have been fertilized with rotted manure or compost. Tamp a 2-inch depression around each plant, forming a saucer to catch the spring rain.*
Watering Instructions: *Water generously for a few days after planting.*
Fertilizing Instructions: *Mix well-rotted manure or compost with soil at planting time. Apply a generous mulch of rotted horse manure over the entire bed after pruning.*
Pruning Instructions: *Cut canes back 1 foot above ground so root system will become established and produce many new canes. Patch should be thinned and pruned in February. Cut canes back to 3 1/2 to 4 1/2 feet high. Cut dead and spindly canes off at ground level.*

Other Information: The ground cannot support too many canes. The secret to producing better berries is due to pruning and thinning. New plants sprout from underground roots and multiply rapidly. Pick a spot where the plants can be kept in bounds by mowing or cultivating.

Mrs. Joseph W. Shertzer, VP
The Lookout Garden Club
Rainelle, West Virginia

WILD FERN FOR ROCK GARDENS

Temperature Zone: *7.*
What To Plant: *Plants gathered with soil.*
How To Plant: *Search the woods for hardy plants that are not too fully developed. Relocate plants in similiar surroundings as found. Ferns can take care of themselves once established.*
Fertilizing Instructions: *Mulch well.*

Other Information: May reestablish a dozen varieties of ferns into a rock garden.

Mrs. Daniel T. Skelton, Past Pres.
Dig N Dream Garden Club
Manchester, Tennessee

IMPATIENS

What To Plant: *Bedding plants.*
When To Plant: *As early as possible after frost.*
Type Of Soil: *Any kind.*
How To Plant: *Plant on north side of house in a rock garden.*
Watering Instructions: *Keep well watered.*

Other Information: Plants may be dug in the fall and brought into house to bloom all winter. Cuttings may be rooted in water and planted outdoors in spring. Mulch over area where plants bloomed outdoors. Many little plants will appear in May and can be transplanted.

Mrs. G. D. Jay, III
Hoe and Grow Garden Club
West Memphis, Arkansas

SMALL JAPANESE GARDEN

Specific Variety: *Low spreading.*
What To Plant: *Shrubs, juniperus, Virginia prostrata, bonsai.*
When To Plant: *Spring.*
Type Of Soil: *Well-drained slightly dry soil.*
How To Plant: *Dig holes large enough to hold root balls.*
Watering Instructions: *Once a week in dry area.*
Fertilizing Instructions: *Peat moss, pine nuggets, stones.*
Pruning Instructions: *Keep bonsai trimmed.*

Other Information: Build a small Japanese garden, using suitable shrubs, lan-

Japanese Garden

terns, washed rocks from stream bed, pine nuggets and stones. Make an attractive area where nothing else will thrive.

Mrs. C. O. Briddell, Past Pres.
Greenway Garden Club
Baltimore, Maryland

SAXIFRAGA UMBROSA

Specific Variety: *London Pride.*
Temperature Zone: *5.*
What To Plant: *Bedding plants or seeds.*
When To Plant: *Early spring.*
Type Of Soil: *Well-drained light soil in rock garden.*
How To Plant: *Dig shallow holes large enough to spread roots.*
Watering Instructions: *Water only if weather is extra dry.*
Fertilizing Instructions: *Plant food may be applied 2 or 3 times during the growing season. Any complete fertilizer may be used. Scatter thinly around plants.*
Pruning Instructions: *Separate plants in early spring when clumps get too heavy.*

Other Information: Foliage is very interesting.

Mrs. Harold Englebardt, Adv.
Woodmere Garden Club
Woodmere, New York

VIRGINIA BLUE BELLS FOR ROCK GARDEN

Temperature Zone: *7.*
What To Plant: *Plants.*
When To Plant: *Early spring.*
Type Of Soil: *Rich soil gathered with plants.*
How To Plant: *Look for plants along the banks of streams. Gather plants with soil. Relocate as soon as possible in garden. Once established, the plants will return year after year.*

Mrs. Daniel T. Skelton, Past Pres.
Dig N Dream Garden Club
Manchester, Tennessee

DRABA REPENS

Specific Variety: *Repens.*
Temperature Zone: *3.*
What To Plant: *Rooted divisions.*
When To Plant: *Anytime during growing season.*
Type Of Soil: *Sandy loam.*
How To Plant: *Cut off a rooted section with edger or trowel; dig a small hole and press into soil to former depth.*
Watering Instructions: *Water when transplanting.*
Pruning Instructions: *Cut out around edges with an edger when plants spread more than desired.*

Other Information: This is a most satisfactory plant for rock gardens. Plant is covered with small bright yellow flowers in early spring. Lovely with scilla and other early bulbs. Prune back below the flowering stems and plant will bloom twice more during the summer.

Irene I. Irwin, Horticultural Chm.
Tamworth Garden Club
Tamworth, New Hampshire

BOTTLE GARDEN

Temperature Zone: *8.*
What To Plant: *Moss, wandering jew.*
When To Plant: *Anytime.*
Type Of Soil: *Standard potting soil.*
How To Plant: *Layer bottom of bottle with charcoal. Use roll of foil or stiff paper to slide soil down into bottle. Prevents soil from getting on sides.*
Watering Instructions: *Needs water very seldom.*
Fertilizing Instructions: *Use plant food at initial planting.*
Pruning Instructions: *Thin out rapidly growing plants if foliage gets too dense.*

Other Information: Select an interesting clean dry bottle. Use wooden spoon handle to cover roots and arrange plant material. Keep bottle gardens in good light, but not direct sunlight as sun rays can burn plants. The bottle garden is hardy and practically takes care of itself. Can sprinkle colored gravel inside to add a touch of color and even match room decor.

Barbara Tubbs, Pres.
Bonita Garden Club
Jones, Louisiana

TERRARIUM

Specific Variety: *Woodland plants or other small plants.*
What To Plant: *Small ferns, galax, ratsvein, small snake plants, any small plants.*
When To Plant: *Anytime plants are available.*
Type Of Soil: *Mixture of peat moss, potting soil and garden soil.*
How To Plant: *Use glass container with cover; put in drainage material. Add soil.*
Watering Instructions: *Sprinkle small amount of water when planting; cover and set aside. Need not water for several months.*

Pruning Instructions: *Pinch off if plants get too large.*

Other Information: Remove cover for a short time if moisture forms on inside of container.

Grace M. Padgett, Sec.
Plant and Pluck Garden Club
Hillsville, Virginia

TERRARIUM

Specific Variety: *Strawberry begonia, ivy, variegated nephthytis.*
Temperature Zone: *7.*
What To Plant: *Small plants.*
When To Plant: *Anytime.*
Type Of Soil: *Barbecue base.*
How To Plant: *Place 2 1/2 to 3 inches of soil mixture in bottom of container. Add water to level of soil; let soak for 30 minutes. Pour off excess water. Set out plants in soil.*
Watering Instructions: *Needs water only when dry.*
Pruning Instructions: *Only prune overgrown larger leaves.*

Other Information: Cut the tops off 1 gallon cider jugs; plant in one half, then put the other bottom on top. Use 3 1-inch strips of scotch tape to hold together. They are very solid.

Dorothy Thompson, Past Pres., Corr. Sec.
Richmond Evergreen Garden Club
Seattle, Washington

TERRARIUM

Temperature Zone: *8.*
What To Plant: *African violets, ferns, moss, ivy, philodendron, begonias, peperomias.*
When To Plant: *Anytime.*
Type Of Soil: *All-purpose potting soil.*
How To Plant: *Place charcoal on bottom of clear container for drainage; add soil. Set out the larger plants first; add smaller*

plants. Leave plants in containers to limit growth. Add moss as top layer.

Watering Instructions: *Wet plants after planting. Put lid on terrarium. Water condensation on the glass will indicate moisture. Remove lid to allow some moisture to escape. Do not water again until soil is dry. This may be for several months.*

Fertilizing Instructions: *May use plant food at initial planting. Not needed again for many months.*

Pruning Instructions: *Prune ivy or plants that get too tall.*

Other Information: Decorate with colored gravel, statues and bark. Never place terrarium in direct sunlight as plants may burn. Try to use same basic shade-loving plants. Fluorescent lights may be used effectively.

Barbara Tubbs, Pres.
Bonita Garden Club
Jones, Louisiana

TERRARIUM

Temperature Zone: *8.*
What To Plant: *Seeds, bedding plants, shrubs, miniature slow-growing plants.*
When To Plant: *Anytime.*
Type of Soil: *Sandy humus.*
How To Plant: *Place small rocks and charcoal in bottom of terrarium; add soil.*
Watering Instructions: *Add enough water to moisten soil when planting. Add a small amount after several days.*
Fertilizing Instructions: *Add a small amount when planting.*
Pruning Instructions: *May be pruned if plants grow too large.*

Other Information: Place terrarium in light. Set out plants in a variety of shapes and sizes.

Mrs. Fred Rossnagel, Sr.
Ridgefield Reapers Garden Club
Montgomery, Alabama

Terrarium

TERRARIUM

Temperature Zone: *3.*
What To Plant: *Baby tears, coleus, fittonia, miniature African violets, ferns, ivy, begonias.*
When To Plant: *Wild plants in fall, cultivated plants anytime.*
Type Of Soil: *2 parts peat moss, 1 part soil, 1 part sand.*
How To Plant: *Line bottom of container with peat moss; add soil mixed with charcoal. Set out plants to create a scene.*
Watering Instructions: *Spray with water lightly about once a month.*
Pruning Instructions: *Trim to keep plants small.*

Other Information: Use a turkey-sized Brown-in-a-Bag to sterilize soil for potting. Add 1/2 to 1 cup of water and bake as you would turkey. Store the soil in the bag until ready to plant.

Mrs. Ted Arnold, Past State Pres.
Milbank Town and Country Garden Club
Twin Brooks, South Dakota

TERRARIUM

Temperature Zone: *3.*
What To Plant: *Ivy, fern, croton, peperomia, moss, lichen or wildings.*
When To Plant: *Anytime.*
Type Of Soil: *Half sandy loam, half leaf mold.*
How To Plant: *Place charcoal and coarse gravel in bottom of container for drainage; add soil. Set out plants.*
Watering Instructions: *Water enough to keep plants growing. Do not get water on leaves.*
Fertilizing Instructions: *Use Hyponex plant food when needed for growth.*
Pruning Instructions: *Keep plants trimmed to desired size.*

Other Information: Plant on slope to give height so all plants may be seen at same time. Place a piece of glass on top to hold the moisture during the day. Open container at night. Keep in a partially light position. Wipe sides dry if too much condensation collects.

Mrs. Harry D. Shryock, Pres.
Big Sky Garden Club
Superior, Montana

HOUSE TERRARIUM

Temperature Zone: *4.*
What To Plant: *Small plants.*
When To Plant: *Anytime.*
Type Of Soil: *Sterile soil mix or coarse sand, peat moss, good loam.*
How To Plant: *Plant using long-handled spoon. Water each plant as you plant.*
Watering Instructions: *Water at planting time. Requires very little water and tamp each plant as you plant them. Try not to get dirt on plants when planting.*
Fertilizing Instructions: *All plants as planted. Cover soil with moss, then water gently with a baster.*
Pruning Instructions: *Pinch out plant tops when too tall.*

Other Information: Place a layer of pebbles or broken pottery in container; cover lightly with 1/2 inch charcoal for small container or 1 inch in larger container. Spoon in dirt, being careful not to get on sides of container. Tamp in until about 1 inch thick. Set out plants; water lightly. Cover container. May remove cover for a short time if moisture condenses. If a plant should die, remove immediately.

Mrs. Paul Mitchell, Past Pres.
Keokuk Garden Club
Keokuk, Iowa

REDBIRD CACTUS (PEDILANTHUS)

Temperature Zone: *7.*
What To Plant: *Bedding plants.*
Type Of Soil: *Garden soil.*
How To Plant: *Clip top of stalk; plant in terrarium.*
Watering Instructions: *Water when dry.*
Pruning Instructions: *Prune to shape plant. Pruned stems may be rooted.*

Other Information: Cut stem short; trim small top leaves and plant directly in terrarium. Will root quickly and grow slowly in terrarium.

Mrs. Harmon T. Rowe
Highland Central Garden Club
Memphis, Tennessee

TERRARIUM

Temperature Zone: *10.*
What To Plant: *Plants from woodland.*
When To Plant: *Anytime.*
Type Of Soil: *Loose humus with leaf mold.*
How To Plant: *Place 1 inch of gravel in bottom of glass container; sprinkle layer of broken charcoal over layer. Add leaf mold and humus.*
Water Instructions: *Sprinkle with water to moisten. Little water is needed when*

glass container is covered.
Pruning Instructions: *Plants should be cut back if they grow too large.*

Other Information: Almost any type of glass container may be used for a successful terrarium. A desert or arid terrarium is started in much the same way as the woodland type, omitting the layer of gravel or charcoal as soil should be sandy. Needs more sun and air.

Mrs. Milton H. Wahl
Canterbury Garden Club
Wilmington, Delaware

TERRARIUM

Specific Variety: *Dracaena, miniature palm, strawberry begonia, peperomia, miniature gloxinia, aluminum plant.*
Temperature Zone: *6.*
What To Plant: *Bedding plants.*
When To Plant: *Anytime.*
Type Of Soil: *Commercial potting soil.*
How To Plant: *Carefully by hand. Allow room in container for some growth.*
Watering Instructions: *Water only when soil feels dry.*
Pruning Instructions: *Prune plants to conform to container size.*

Other Information: Requires little attention when properly cared for. Keep planting hole 80 percent covered to retain moisture and humidity.

Mrs. Atmur Stokes, Proj. Com. Co-Chm.
Henderson County Garden Club
Henderson, Kentucky

TERRARIUM

Temperature Zone: *9.*
What To Plant: *Small plants, peperomia, ferns, ivy, prayer plants.*
When To Plant: *Anytime.*
Type Of Soil: *Sterilized planting soil and charcoal.*

How To Plant: *Add 1 inch of charcoal to bottom of bowl; fill with soil until bowl is 1/3 full.*
Watering Instructions: *Water until soil is moist for planting. Use sprinkling bottle to water plants.*
Fertilizing Instructions: *Very little.*
Pruning Instructions: *Do not disturb roots any more than possible when planting.*

Other Information: May use bottles, fish bowls or brandy snifters for planting. Keep in north window. Never let the sun shine on glass or the plants will burn. Cover the top with a glass lid or cork and watering will not be necessary. Hang glass ball in a macrame net, if desired.

Mrs. M. H. Morris, Pres.
Leaburg Garden Club
Leaburg, Oregon

TERRARIUM

Temperature Zone: *8.*
What To Plant: *Iris Moss, Baby Tears, Fairy Fern, Boston Fern.*
When To Plant: *Anytime.*
Type Of Soil: *1 part sand, 1 part peat moss, 3 parts leaf mold. Good mellow loam.*
How To Plant: *Wash glass container with chlorine solution 2 or 3 days before planting. Place small rocks in bottom of container. Combine 1 ounce of charcoal and 1 pint of sand. Pour over rock layer. Add soil mixture. Press plant roots firmly into soil. Place moss around plants. Add 1 ounce of water; close terrarium.*
Pruning Instructions: *Tape a razer blade to a stick. Prune plants when necessary.*

Other Information: Cook garden soil in a 325-degree oven for 1 hour. Cool and sift; place in terrarium with tender loving care.

Mrs. W. G. Boles, Sec.
The Annie B. Walker Garden Club
Hardaway, Alabama

Houseplants

The raising of plants indoors has become so popular in America today that it is virtually impossible to find an office or home which does not boast at least one green plant.

Almost everyone enjoys the charm and freshness of these botanical additions to the home and office decor. And, since plants suitable for indoor use are so varied in size, shape, leaf pattern and color, the modern decorator will have no trouble in selecting gorgeous plants for any decorating scheme.

When selecting plants for your own home, it is important to consider many things. Make sure you consider the ultimate size and shape of the plant and its requirements for heat, light, water, humidity and food.

Remember, the success of a houseplant depends not only on where it is placed in your interior decorating plan, but also on how it is treated. In other words, in order for the plant to maintain its luscious green color and abundant foliage, you must provide the things necessary for it to live in an indoor atmosphere.

Light is essential for almost all plant life. Some plants require no direct sunlight and only very little light of any kind. These plants are ideal for areas in your home or office that are relatively dark.

Other plants require some indirect sunlight and are grown successfully

African Violets

near windows or doors. And, still others must have some direct sunlight and can only thrive on porches, patios or windowsills. This need for light is a primary consideration when selecting a plant for a particular spot in your home.

Thought should also be given to temperature and air circulation. Most plants need fresh air—avoid placing plants in small rooms where people smoke a lot. Also, consider the normal temperature of the room—most plants require a moderate temperature range and will not do well in either extreme.

Be sure to water your plants properly. Remember—almost all plants need to be kept moist *not* wet. Do not let the soil dry completely. And, above all—do not water your plants with cold tap water. Use only room temperature water so that the plant's roots will not suffer from the change in temperature and become stunted.

Remember that the best pot for almost any houseplant is an ordinary earthenware pot. If you want to use a colorful outside container that will complement both the plant and the decor, leave the plant in its original earthenware container and place it in the decorative holder. Plastic pots are cheaper, and plants usually do well in them. But, do not use a glazed pot for any kind of plant.

If this is your first attempt in the cultivation of houseplants, be sure to select a species that requires minimum attention and little light, such as a philodendron or a sanseviera. Leave the growing of African Violets until you have learned and experimented with the easier varieties. You'll be much happier with a healthy, attractive cactus than a rather sickly Maidenhair Fern.

HOUSEPLANTS

Flowering Houseplants

African Violets	Episcias	Hibiscus
Amaryllis	Flowering Maple	Lipstick Plant
Begonia	Fuchsias	Plumbago
Bird of Paradise	Gardenia	Shrimp Plant
Bromeliad	Geranium	Sweet Olive
Cacti	Ginger	Temple Bells
Clivia	Gloxinia	Wax Plant

Foliage Plants — No Direct Light Required

Asparagus Fern	Hatrack Plant	Pothos
Aspidistra	Holly Fern	Sansevieria
Boston Fern	Monstera	Screw Pine
Chinese Evergreen	Palm	Spathiphyllum
Dracaena	Philodendron	Spider Plant
Grape Ivy	Pony Tail Plant	Syngonium

Foliage Plants — Filtered Light

Avocado	Pellionia	Pteris Fern
Baby's Tears	Pilea	Rubber Plant
Dieffenbachia	Pittosporum	Schefflera
English Ivy	Podocarpus	Swedish Ivy
Norfolk Island Pine	Polystichum Fern	Umbrella Plant
Ophiopogon	Prayer Plant	Weeping Fig

SICK HOUSEPLANTS

SYMPTOMS	PROBABLE CAUSES
Leaves turn crisp and brown	temperature too high; humidity too low; moisture content not stable
Leaves yellow and drop off	temperature too extreme; use of cold water; lack of plant food or fertilizer
Leaves wilt	not enough light; too small a container
No flowers	not enough sunlight; humidity too low; wrong kind of fertilizer
Flower buds drop off	temperature too high; humidity too low
Spots on leaves and stems	use of cold water; hot sunshine on leaves

REMEDIES:

1. Always water your plants with room temperature tap water.
2. Never expose a plant to a drastic temperature change.
3. Pick off all dead and faded flowers immediately.
4. Wipe or mist the foliage once a week with tepid water.
5. Keep the moisture content of the soil even.
6. Fertilize regularly with a name brand fertilizer.
7. Make sure your plants get enough light (sun or indirect).
8. Transplant when pot becomes too small for the root system.

AFRICAN VIOLET PLANTING FOR APARTMENT LIVING

Temperature Zone: *3.*
What To Plant: *Plants.*
How To Plant: *Punch holes in bottoms of plastic squatty glasses with a hot cork-screw. Tear foam-type egg cartons into small pieces; place in bottoms of glasses for good drainage. Add soil and set the plants out in glasses. Place the plants in foam-type trays obtained from packaged meats in grocery store. Place on a Flora Cart under individual fluorescent lights. Pour water into the foam-type trays to increase humidity.*

Mrs. Frederick Johns, VP
Anchorage Garden Club
Anchorage, Alaska

AFRICAN VIOLETS (SAINT PAULIAS)

Specific Variety: *Grandiflora.*
Temperature Zone: *6.*
What To Plant: *Plant.*
When To Plant: *Anytime.*
Type Of Soil: *Potting mixture plus clean peat moss.*
How To Plant: *Plant in 4 or 5-inch pots to start. Replant in larger pots as plant grows.*
Watering Instructions: *Needs plenty of moisture, preferably from bottom of pot.*
Fertilizing Instructions: *Water soluble 5-10-5, 13-26-13 or 15-30-15.*
Pruning Instructions: *Divide and repot when there is more than one plant in pot.*

Other Information: Soil must be kept moist, not wet or powdery dry. Warm humid air is best. Needs some sunlight about 2 hours daily in winter. Needs strong light all the time.

Mrs. Maud Schmuck, Tel Com.
Plain Dirt Gardeners
Newport, Arkansas

AFRICAN VIOLETS

Specific Variety: *Pink Lady.*
Temperature Zone: *4.*
What To Plant: *Plants or rooted leaves.*
When To Plant: *Set plants out anytime; root leaf cuttings in March.*
Type Of Soil: *Good humus soil and peat moss.*
How To Plant: *Plant firmly in soil.*
Watering Instructions: *Roots want a fair amount of water. Do not splash water on leaves or crown.*
Fertilizing Instructions: *Feed once a month with Hyponex.*
Pruning Instructions: *Keep dead flowers and leaves pulled off.*

Other Information: Leaf cuttings put in boxes of sand or water and under glass will grow to flowering size in about 8 months.

Mrs. John Wittich, Pres.
Keokuk Garden Club
Keokuk, Iowa

AFRICAN VIOLETS

Specific Variety: *Miriam Steele.*
What To Plant: *Leaf cuttings.*
Type Of Soil: *Loose soil.*
How To Plant: *Root the cuttings in water, vermiculite or perlite after cuttings show good growth and have put up leaves from base of plant. Repot in loose soil.*
Watering Instructions: *Do not overwater. Plants respond to wicking. Place pots with wicks over container of water mixed with fertilizer and trace elements. Keep wick in solution all the time.*
Fertilizing Instructions: *Hyponex, African Violet food, Blue Whale in solution.*

Other Information: Sunlight should never be used on white variety, even in winter. Indirect light is best.

Mrs. John Burroughs, Area Reading Chm.
Portales Garden Club
Portales, New Mexico

AFRICAN VIOLETS

Specific Variety: *Tommy Lou, variegated varieties.*
Temperature Zone: *6.*
What To Plant: *Freshly cut leaves.*
When To Plant: *Spring.*
Type Of Soil: *Equal amounts of peat moss and vermiculite.*
How To Plant: *Insert leaves in growing media after dipping in rooting powder in closed clear plastic container.*
Watering Instructions: *Keep moist but not wet.*
Fertilizing Instructions: *Fertilize with 5-50-17 when plants are well established.*

Other Information: *Variegated leaf violets do best with less light than other violets. Grow under fluorescent lights with 1 Gro-Lux tube and 1 cool white 40 watt, about 12 inches from the light. Leave lights on 15 hours a day.*

Margaret Buckner, VP
Clarksville Garden Club
Clarksville, Tennessee

AFRICAN VIOLETS

Specific Variety: *Blue Palm, double or single bloom pinks, violet, white.*
Temperature Zone: *3.*
What To Plant: *Rooted leaves.*
When To Plant: *All year.*
Type Of Soil: *2 parts peat moss to 1 part coarse sand.*
How To Plant: *Mix soil well; plant in 5 or 6-inch pots with good drainage.*
Watering Instructions: *Do not overwater. Plants do well if placed, in their pots, into container of moist peat moss to absorb moisture. Use tepid water for watering.*
Fertilizing Instructions: *Violet fertilizer only.*
Pruning Instructions: *Remove leaves from large plants to make uniform.*

Other Information: Keep soil dry for a period of 4 to 6 weeks until more flower buds appear, then return to normal watering. This method will produce several flowerings in a season. Plants like a temperature of 55 degrees and a shaded place. Most any window with a filtered light will do well.

Mrs. Henry Wessels
Klemme Federated Garden Club
Klemme, Iowa

AFRICAN VIOLETS

Temperature Zone: *2.*
What To Plant: *Leaves or rooted plants.*
When To Plant: *Anytime.*
Type Of Soil: *Porous.*
How To Plant: *Root leaves in vermiculite in closed container, keeping moist. Transplant into African violet soil in pots when baby plants form around leaves. Keep covered with plastic until plants are well-rooted. Must have indirect light.*
Watering Instructions: *Wicks and reservoirs for dry soil.*
Fertilizing Instructions: *Once a week with violet fertilizer.*
Pruning Instructions: *As needed.*

Other Information: Rotate pots; remove dead blossoms.

Mrs. Delmer E. Johnson, Master Judge
Community Garden Club of Alamosa
Alamosa, Colorado

AFRICAN VIOLETS

Type Of Soil: *Loose humus-type soil.*
Watering Instructions: *Water with warm water, taking care not to get centers wet.*
Fertilizing Instructions: *Use 1/4 of the recommended amount of fertilizer when watering.*

Other Information: Place violets in a window to get the morning sun. Keep at a temperature of between 65 and 70 degrees.

Mrs. Edd Bussell, Hist.
Frenchman Valley Garden Club
Imperial, Nebraska

ASPIDISTRA

Specific Variety: *Elatior.*
Temperature Zone: *8.*
What To Plant: *Divided root stock.*
When To Plant: *Spring.*
Type Of Soil: *Ordinary.*
How To Plant: *Plant roots about 6 inches deep. May be planted under a tree.*
Watering Instructions: *Every few days until plant is well established. Takes little care after the first year.*
Fertilizing Instructions: *In spring with any type fertilizer.*
Pruning Instructions: *Cut brown leaves back. Multiplies rapidly.*

Other Information: The leaves last for weeks in an arrangement. They are pretty all year-round in the garden. Will grow in poor soil and in part shade. The leaves dry very well when cut while still green and placed in jar to dry.

Mrs. H. W. Lingham, Pres.
Woodbine Garden Club
Jackson, Mississippi

AMARYLLIS
(HIPPEASTRUM)

Specific Variety: *Hybrid houseplant varieties.*
What To Plant: *Bulbs.*
When To Plant: *Late fall, winter or early spring.*
Type Of Soil: *2 parts loam, 1 part peat moss or leaf mold, 1/2 to 1 part sand.*
How To Plant: *Allow 2 inches space between bulb and container walls. Set bulb so that half of it is above the soil.*
Watering Instructions: *Sparingly or none when first potted until growth starts. Copiously during growing period.*
Fertilizing Instructions: *Biweekly applications of liquid houseplant fertilizer.*

Other Information: Cease watering in September. Store, in pot, in cool place 50 to 60 degrees. Renew top inch of soil with fresh mixture when flower bud appears beside leaf growth, not within it. Place in good light and moisten. Complete repotting necessary every 3 or 4 years.

Mrs. Marcus M. Finley, Pres.
Perennial, Rose Gardeners Clubs
El Dorado, Arkansas

BIRD OF PARADISE

Specific Variety: *Strelitzia Reginea.*
Temperature Zone: *8.*
What To Plant: *Pot plant.*
When To Plant: *Anytime.*
Type Of Soil: *Rich potting soil mixed with peat moss.*
How To Plant: *Place in soil in pot with drainage holes.*
Watering Instructions: *Water when soil feels dry to touch.*
Fertilizing Instructions: *Fertilize moderately and regularly.*

Other Information: Needs plenty of light but not necessarily sun. Repot in larger container as plant grows and roots have filled the pot. Plant likes high humidity. Allow to rest during winter by watering and feeding less.

Mrs. Jack Windsor, Pres.
Hilltop Garden Club
Montgomery, Alabama

BIRD OF PARADISE

Specific Variety: *Strelitzia Reginea.*
Temperature Zone: *7.*
What To Plant: *Seeds.*
When To Plant: *Seed may be started at any season.*
Type Of Soil: *Rich soil with adequate drainage.*
How To Plant: *After plant is started in pot, transplant to a tub as it will not bloom until some size, at least ten leaves.*
Watering Instructions: *Only a moderate amount in winter. Do not take out of pot or tub in summer. Sink to rim in garden and feed.*

Fertilizing Instructions: *Do not feed in winter as the plant is semidormant. Feed regularly in summer. Liquid plant food is satisfactory.*
Pruning Instructions: *Remove dying leaves.*

Other Information: Blooms generally in late summer or fall. Winter temperature 45 to 50 degrees. Cool porch is satisfactory. Drainage is important. Can be kept on wet stones if kept in house in winter. This will increase humidity. Suitable for home greenhouse but can be winter stored in home. Abundant light needed. Not necessarily full sun. Semishade.

Ida S. Phillips, Horticulture Chm.
Sussex Gardeners
Rehoboth Beach, Delaware

SUCCULENTS

Specific Variety: *Any variety.*
Temperature Zone: *2.*
When To Plant: *Keep cacti in greenhouse in winter.*
Type Of Soil: *Well-drained sandy loam.*
How To Plant: *Clay pots with pebbles*

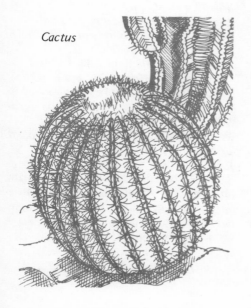

Cactus

and good drainage. Leave 5/8-inch space at top for adequate water.
Watering Instructions: *About once a week in winter, 4 or 5 days in summer.*
Fertilizing Instructions: *Not usually necessary. Cacti can be killed by ordinary amounts of fertilizer.*

Other Information: Spray for mealy bugs with 1/2 strength Malathion and water every 4 or 5 days. Succulents cannot stand strong aerosol sprays. Dipping in Malathion mix is good. Spray or dip containers and shelves as mealy bugs often nest on lips and bottoms of containers.

Pamela Linn, Sec.
Saco Flower Farmers
Saco, Montana

CACTUS

Specific Variety: *Golden stars.*
Temperature Zone: *8.*
What To Plant: *Plants, small leaves or cuttings.*
When To Plant: *Preferably in spring.*
Type Of Soil: *Sandy loam in dry condition, porous soil.*
How To Plant: *Place broken pieces of clay pots in bottom of container to allow proper drainage. Place plant in soil.*
Watering Instructions: *Water only when soil becomes dry. Water sparingly in winter since plants are dormant.*
Fertilizing Instructions: *Good houseplant food such as Hyponex. Use sparingly during spring and summer.*
Pruning Instructions: *Requires no pruning.*

Other Information: Common table salt may be sprinkled on hands to remove most of the thorns after potting and handling cactus. Gloves should be worn. Bright showy flowers when plants have grown considerably.

Mrs. John O. Davis, Treas.
Canterbury Bells Garden Club
Montgomery, Alabama

Coleus

COLEUS BLUMEI

Temperature Zone: *10.*
What To Plant: *Bedding plants or seedlings.*
When To Plant: *May 1.*
Type Of Soil: *Porous, well-drained soil.*
How To Plant: *Set plants out about 8 to 10 inches apart.*
Watering Instructions: *Keep ground moist.*
Fertilizing Instructions: *4 parts cottonseed and 1 part blood meal. Feed July 4 and Labor Day.*
Pruning Instructions: *Pinch back from time to time to promote bushy growth.*

Other Information: These plants have colored, handsome foliage and grow as high as 2 to 3 feet. Needs morning or late afternoon sun and noonday shade. Cover newly set out plants with strawberry baskets to prevent snails from eating. Use snail bait also.

Mrs. W. R. Wright
Year Around Garden Club
Whittier, California

CYCLAMEN

Specific Variety: *Neapolitanum.*
What To Plant: *Seed or bulbs.*
When To Plant: *Bulbs in spring, seeds in fall.*
Type Of Soil: *Light woodsy soil.*
How To Plant: *Plant bulbs with round sides down. The hollow side is the top of the bulb and the flowers spring from the hollow. Plant just the depth of the bulb. Seed should be just lightly covered.*
Watering Instructions: *Keep bed moist but well drained.*
Fertilizing Instructions: *Cottonseed or bone meal.*

Other Information: Makes beautiful ground cover in either sun or shade.

Cora Miller
Kennydale Garden Club
Renton, Washington

FALSE ARALIA

Specific Variety: *Dizygotheca elegantissima.*
Temperature Zone: *8.*
What To Plant: *Small plant about 12 inches tall.*
When To Plant: *Any season.*
Type Of Soil: *Any good potting soil.*
How To Plant: *In large pot with 1 inch left at top above soil line.*
Watering Instructions: *Water well in warm weather. Keep fairly dry in winter.*
Fertilizing Instructions: *About every 4 months following instructions on fertilizer container.*
Pruning Instructions: *Only to shape plant into desired pattern outline.*

Other Information: Hardy indoor plant that requires semishade in summer but a bright spot in winter. Humid conditions are preferred but not essential. Plant grows slowly and has lovely foliage.

Mrs. Thomas M. Miller, Pres.
Daffodil Garden Club of Alabama
Dothan, Alabama

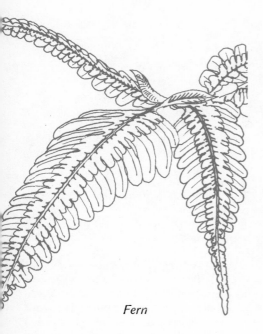

Fern

OUTDOOR FERNS

Specific Variety: *Christmas, Cinnamon, Maidenhair, Ebony Spleenwort.*
Temperature Zone: *9.*
What To Plant: *Dormant crowns.*
When To Plant: *Fall, winter or very early spring.*
Type Of Soil: *Good garden soil mixed with compost, peat moss and mulch.*
How To Plant: *Never plant any deeper than crown was growing. Hold rhizomes in place with rocks until established, if necessary.*
Watering Instructions: *Do not allow to become dry. Watering during drought conditions imperative.*
Fertilizing Instructions: *Light application of dry sheep manure once a year. Wood ashes may be scattered on bed several times a year. Never use inorganic fertilizer.*
Pruning Instructions: *Cut off dead fronds in late fall.*

Other Information: A fern garden is the best solution for that too shady spot on north side. Once established it is almost carefree. Can rescue beautiful specimens where roads or developments are planned. Ask for permission. Many kinds will live as long as 20 years.

Mrs. Charles A. Pratt, Pres.
Dunes Garden Club
Wilmington, North Carolina

ASPARAGUS FERN

Specific Variety: *Asparagus Sprengeri.*
Temperature Zone: *6.*
What To Plant: *Seeds.*
When To Plant: *February or March.*
Type Of Soil: *Well-drained light soil.*
How To Plant: *May be repotted in hanging baskets when seedlings are 3 to 4 inches high.*
Watering Instructions: *Water biweekly. Soil must be well drained. Loss of leaves may occur if overwatered.*
Fertilizing Instructions: *Use 10-10-10 lightly once in spring and ureaform fertilizer as needed to maintain green color.*

Other Information: Asparagus fern is an excellent plant for hanging baskets. The long stems have narrow leaves and bear small white flowers which are followed by small red berries. It may be grown as an indoor plant during the winter months and placed on the porch in partial shade in summer.

Mrs. Robert G. Thress, Pres.
West Ridge Garden Club
Morristown, Tennessee

HOW TO MAKE FERNS GREENER

Water ferns with 1 teaspoon of household ammonia added to 1 quart of water for rich green color.

Mrs. J. W. ONeal
Lea Olive Garden Club
Montgomery, Alabama

BIRD'S NEST FERN
(ASPLENIUM NIDUS-AVIS)

Temperature Zone: *8.*
What To Plant: *Plants.*
Type Of Soil: *Alkaline soil mixed with peat moss.*
How To Plant: *Buy plant at local nursery when small and keep repotting as plant grows larger.*
Watering Instructions: *Too much moisture will cause loss of color.*
Fertilizing Instructions: *House plant fertilizer once a month.*
Pruning Instructions: *Cut outside fronds and bird's nest found in center.*

Other Information: Use as house plant in winter and may be placed outside in shady location in summer. Leaves are broad and delicate green. Strong sunlight will spot the leaves.

Mrs. Ed Rankin, Treas.
Ridge Acres Garden Club
Montgomery, Alabama

NIGHT BLOOMING CEREUS

Temperature Zone: *4.*
What To Plant: *Slips.*
When To Plant: *Anytime.*
Type Of Soil: *Garden soil.*
How To Plant: *Place small stones in bottom of plant jar and fill with soil.*
Watering Instructions: *Water when dry but do not soak.*
Pruning Instructions: *Cut off any dead leaves after plant blossoms.*

Other Information: Grows well in a south window. Dust occasionally with a wool cloth to keep the leaves clean. Plant starts to blossom about 8 or 9 o'clock at night and stays open until 4 or 5 in the morning. The flower is gorgeous.

Dorcas Ball, W and M Chm.
Homer Garden Club
Homer, Michigan

CHINESE EVERGREEN
(AGLAONEMA)

Specific Variety: *Commutatum.*
Temperature Zone: *8.*
What To Plant: *Rooted cuttings.*
Type Of Soil: *2 parts top soil, 1 part peat moss, 1 part sand.*
How To Plant: *Plant in holes large enough to spread roots. Cover well with soil, pressing firmly around roots.*
Watering Instructions: *Keep evenly moist.*
Fertilizing Instructions: *Small amount of 5-10-5, tobacco ashes.*
Pruning Instructions: *Cut only when stem gets too long.*

Other Information: Direct sun not needed. Place in east or north window. Flowers resemble calla lily. This is a very good apartment dweller's plant. The plant is from Ceylon and originally grew in the forest. Plant has attractive foliage all year.

Juanita W. Lewis
Oakdale Garden Club
Norfolk, Virginia

ORCHIDS

Specific Variety: *Cymbidium.*
Temperature Zone: *10.*
What To Plant: *Back bulb showing live eye.*
When To Plant: *February through May.*
Type Of Soil: *Light well-drained acid soil.*
How To Plant: *1/3 of depth at 45-degree angle. Do not overpot; roots need to be crowded.*
Watering Instructions: *Needs to be kept moist but not wet. Spray lightly often until plant becomes established.*
Fertilizing Instructions: *Do not fertilize until plant has good leaf growth. Use high nitrogen fertilizer 30-10-10 the first year.*

Other Information: Plant should flower in 3 years. Needs at least 60 percent sun. Plant can stand summer heat but needs cool nights. Can stand 28 degrees for a short time without damage. Use 30-10-10 fertilizer on mature plants for foliage growth and 6-30-30 for flower spikes January to August. Use Malathion or Cygon to control pests.

Mrs. Dana F. Collins
Year Around Garden Club
Whittier, California

PALM

Specific Variety: *Cocos plumosa.*
Temperature Zone: *9.*
What To Plant: *Tree or seeds.*
When To Plant: *Tree in January or February and seeds in September or October.*
Type Of Soil: *General purpose potting mixture.*
How To Plant: *Seeds 1/2 inch deep and tree to depth according to size.*
Watering Instructions: *Keep seeds moist but do not overwater.*
Fertilizing Instructions: *8-8-8 or liquid manure every few weeks during active growing season.*

Other Information: Do not be disappointed in the appearance of the seedlings. Palms are very unattractive in young state with no hint of what they will be like when grown. Will take about a year for seeds to germinate. Palms do not resent being pot bound. This tends to reduce their size, which makes them ideal for indoors. Need plenty of light.

Mrs. R. J. Heaney, Pres.
Louisiana Garden Club Federation
New Orleans, Louisiana

RED-HOT CATTAIL
(ACALYPHA HISPIDA)

Temperature Zone: *6.*
What To Plant: *Plant.*
When To Plant: *Anytime.*
Type Of Soil: *Ordinary good well-drained potting soil.*
How To Plant: *Fill pot with sterile soil; spread roots out and cover well.*

Watering Instructions: *Needs more water than most plants.*
Fertilizing Instructions: *Ra-Pid-Gro every 3 weeks.*
Pruning Instructions: *Keep pruned in a round shape. Root cuttings, if desired.*

Other Information: Plant should be kept in a sunny window in filtered sun. Spray for red spider mites. This plant is truly a conversation piece and is always in bloom. The tails are 22 to 26 inches long.

Mrs. Judson Meyers
Madonna Garden Club
Chattanooga, Tennessee

SCENTED LEAF GERANIUM

Specific Variety: *Attar of Roses, Peppermint, Nutmeg, Cinnamon, Old-Fashioned Rose, Lemon, Lime, Apple, Coconut.*
Temperature Zone: *4.*
What To Plant: *Seeds or cuttings.*
When To Plant: *Seeds in January, cuttings in August.*
Type Of Soil: *Mix 4 parts soil, 4 parts peat moss and 2 parts Vermiculite or Perlite together in baking container. Pour in water until water shows around edge. Bake in preheated 350-degree oven for 1 hour. The soil will smell like a potato baking. A small amount of whiting may be added to acid soil.*
How To Plant: *Cut stem straight across just below leaf. Let cuttings dry for 2 to 3 hours before planting. Let cutting touch bottom of shallow pot for quick rooting. Keep tops covered with moist cloth to prevent leaf wilting.*
Watering Instructions: *When top of soil feels dry to touch.*
Fertilizing Instructions: *Very little.*
Pruning Instructions: *As desired. Some varieties can be pruned to topiary or ornamental shapes.*

Pauline S. Arwood, VP
Longs Peak Garden Club
Longmont, Colorado

POINSETTIAS

Specific Variety: *Any type.*
Temperature Zone: *6.*
When To Plant: *Transfer to good potting soil after leaves shed.*
Type Of Soil: *Small amount of sand in potting soil.*
How To Plant: *Transfer as for any type plant. Plant outside after danger of frost is over. Plant at same level as in pot.*
Watering Instructions: *Water well at least once a week.*
Pruning Instructions: *Cut back almost to the ground, when planting.*

Other Information: Usually blooms all winter and spring. Must be fertilized, if blooms are desired.

Helen Collins
Colonial Garden Club
Bristol, Virginia

SCHEFFLERA

Temperature Zone: *6.*
Type Of Soil: *Rich garden soil.*
How To Plant: *Plant in 8-inch pot; place pot in larger container filled with peat moss or sawdust.*
Watering Instructions: *Water well twice a week. Excess water drains into larger container.*
Fertilizing Instructions: *Water with 1 tablespoon fish fertilizer to 1 quart of water once a month.*
Pruning Instructions: *Additional sprouts at bottom of plant may be removed.*

Other Information: Does well as entry plant inside on east side. Likes light but not sun.

Kay Kirby
Jefferson County Garden Club
Madras, Oregon

SCHEFFLERA

Temperature Zone: *8.*
When To Plant: *Anytime.*

Type Of Soil: *Potting soil mixed with good garden soil and a small amount vermiculite.*
How To Plant: *Plant in a large pot as Schefflera grows quite large. Cover just the roots well but not the stem as plant will suffocate.*
Watering Instructions: *Water thoroughly about every 2 weeks, taking care not to let the roots get soggy.*
Fertilizing Instructions: *Mix 1 teaspoon of fish emulsion with about 1 quart of warm water and fertilize twice a year.*
Pruning Instructions: *Cut plant off about 12 inches if too leggy; set out cut part in pot to make another plant.*

Other Information: Mix a little chelated iron in some warm water and water thoroughly if leaves turn yellow. Plant needs indirect light.

Mrs. Julian Hancock
Canterbury Bells Garden Club
Alternate Federation Dir.
Montgomery, Alabama

SEA ONION
(ORNITHOGALUM)

Specific Variety: *Caudatum.*
Temperature Zone: *6.*
What to Plant: *Bulbs*
Type Of Soil: *Good garden loam.*
How To Plant: *Press bulbs halfway into soil.*
Watering Instructions: *Keep moist until leaflet appears, then water thoroughly only when top of soil is dry.*
Fertilizing Instructions: *Any houseplant fertilizer.*
Pruning Instructions: *Leaves may be cut to desired length and they will curl under attractively.*

Other Information: As the bulb grows it pushes up out of the soil with only the roots underneath. The outer brown skin can be removed and the satiny green exposed. Small bulblets form and often drop and take root. Plant is a medicinal herb. The crushed leaf is useful in treating minor burns and cuts.

Mrs. Harold G. Phillips
Pub. Rel. Chm., Immediate Past Pres.
Garden Club of Wyoming Valley
Kingston, Pennsylvania

SPATHIPHYLLUM

Specific Variety: *S. Wallisii.*
What To Plant: *Division of roots.*
When To Plant: *Early spring.*
Type Of Soil: *Rich soil.*
How To Plant: *Division of roots in pots in early spring.*
Watering Instructions: *Keep soil damp until roots have taken well. Needs ample water in hot weather.*
Fertilizing Instructions: *Fertilize regularly with diluted liquid fertilizer during growing season.*

Other Information: These plants like very humid conditions and filtered light. They do very well inside with less light. Temperature in winter should be at least 55 degrees. Let pots become fairly rootbound. Keep moist and fertilize regularly. Plant makes a most beautiful waxy leaf houseplant. A plant in a 12-inch pot will give dozens of flowers.

Mrs. H. L. Pentecost, Pres.
Rake and Hoe Garden Club
Lake Charles, Louisiana

UMBRELLA PLANT
(CYPERUS PAPYRUS)

Temperature Zone: *7.*
What To Plant: *Whole root system.*
When To Plant: *Early spring.*
Type Of Soil: *Acid.*
How To Plant: *Dig hole; pour in water. Set out plant, tamping down firmly.*
Watering Instructions: *Water at least every other day.*
Fertilizing Instructions: *Organic compost.*
Pruning Instructions: *Do not prune but cut stems when they show signs of yellowing at end. Clip to short length; invert and root in water for another plant.*

Other Information: May be grown outdoors in warmer climates. Bring in house in winter in cooler climates. A spade should be inserted through the root system of a large plant to cut as much as desired for a house plant. The strong long stems will stay green and upright all winter if watered often. Plant in a can with several holes in the bottom; place in an ornamental container. There is nothing prettier for flower arranging than this plant for line, either clipped, bent or natural.

Mrs. Harmon T. Rowe
Highland Central Garden Club
National Inter-Federation Relations Chm.
Memphis, Tennessee

HOW TO PROPAGATE
DIEFFENBACHIAS

Specific Variety: *Picta Memoria.*
Temperature Zone: *8.*
What To Plant: *Segments of stem.*
When To Plant: *When plant becomes tall and leggy.*
Type Of Soil: *Sand, sphagnum moss or mixture of both.*
How To Plant: *Cut stem between each node; insert segments horizontally into rooting medium.*
Watering Instructions: *Keep medium moist, not wet.*
Fertilizing Instructions: *Liquid fertilizer.*

Other Information: Keep stems shaded and in a warm place until rooting occurs. This will take many weeks. Plant is then ready to be planted in container. Needs low to medium light. Leaves burn if humidity is low. Avoid drafty location. Keep soil well-drained but uniformly moist.

Mrs. S. M. Watkins, Jr., Pres.
Woodland Garden Club
Henderson, North Carolina

Index

PHOTOGRAPHY CREDITS: Cover: Bellingrath Gardens; Interior Photography: W. Atlee Burpee Company; Bellingrath Gardens; Sunnyside Nurseries — R. Holtkamp; Yoder Brothers, Inc.; Callaway Gardens; Ferry-Morse Seed Company Inc.; Rockline.

From Garden Club Members

New Gardening Book Complements The Garden Club Cooking And Entertainment Library!

Favorite Ways to Garden -- From Garden Flowers to House Plants, Shrubs to Roses, or to Special Gardens of many kinds . . . here is a compilation of Gardening techniques, personally developed by Garden Club members, sure to be of equal interest to the experienced and novice gardener!

New Desserts Cookbook -- Whether flaming crepes, sherbets, or frosted cakes -- desserts add the crowning touch to night or noonday meals! This marvelous book contains hundreds of tempting desserts, sure to bring smiles of delight from young and old alike!

All Purpose Cookbook -- Here are found main dishes, desserts, salads, snacks . . . recipes for every meal you can imagine. This attractive combination cookbook makes meal planning and preparation easy, fun, and guarantees success every time!

Casseroles Cookbook -- From Poultry to sirloin tips, here are hundreds of delicious and timesaving casseroles. Mix 'n match vegetables, meats, pasta, seasonings . . . and come up with a scrumptious meal, all in one dish. Fun to prepare and a breeze to serve!

Meats Cookbook -- It is said that "Meat Makes the Meal!" Surely nothing beats roast beef, lamb, pork, veal . . . or any other meat dish. Plain or fancy, mouth watering main dishes for every taste and occasion are included in this valuable recipe book.

TRIED AND PROVEN GARDENING TECHNIQUES

--from America's most experienced gardeners!

Here are complete gardening *methods,* not tips, perfected by America's Garden Club members -- assuring success every time! Each technique has been painstakingly developed and proven to work for its contributor. No detail, from planting to pruning, has been omitted! And these **Favorite Ways to Garden** came from gardeners who truly care about gardening, and know how to do the job right!

Favorite Ways to Garden is the something "new and different" that is perfect for hard-to-buy-for friends and relatives, no matter *where* their gardens grow -- North, South, East, or West! An easy-to-follow Climatic Zone Map shows the correct temperature zone for the various gardening methods, along with a chart showing the limits of the Average Annual Minimum Temperatures for each of these Climatic Zones outlined on the Map.

When ordering this attractive gardening guide, **Favorite Ways to Garden,** be sure to remember to get a plentiful supply of *Garden Club Cookbooks* -- each recipe personally tested in homes of Garden Club members throughout the country.

Remember birthdays, anniversaries, weddings, holidays, or almost any special occasion with **The New Desserts Cookbook, All Purpose Cookbook, Casseroles Cookbook, Meats Cookbook,** and of course -- the newest book in the Garden Club collection, **Favorite Ways to Garden!**